LOOKING, WORKING, LIVING TERRIFIC 24 HOURS A DAY

LOOKING, WORKING, LIVING TERRIFIC 24 HOURS A DAY

Emily Cho
and Hermine Lueders
Illustrated by Cheryl Lickona

BALLANTINE BOOKS • NEW YORK

Published in the United States by Ballantine Books, a division of
Random House, Inc., New York, and simultaneously in Canada by
Random House of Canada Limited, Toronto.

Designed by Giorgetta Bell McRee

Library of Congress Catalog Card Number: 83-90067
ISBN 0-345-30938-3
This edition published by arrangement with G.P. Putnam's Sons,
New York

Manufactured in the United States of America
First Ballantine Books Trade Edition: September 1983

10 9 8 7 6 5 4 3 2 1

To my mother,
the one who really knows the art of living.

ACKNOWLEDGMENTS

To the many women I interviewed—all willing to share the answers
they'd found and each still looking for more.
To all my clients who have used the New Image service to ease their
personal lives—and let me enjoy with them the thrill of change.
To Neila for her wonderful contribution and support.
To Diane and Owen, who once again have made the whole process
of writing a book a shared adventure.

CONTENTS

What is image? Do clothes ever lie? • *Should you care?* • *Breaking into the winner's circle* • *Is your body getting in your way?* • *Can clothes matter too much?* • *How different women use their image* • *Who do you think you are? (Or don't you know?)* • *Intriguing or disturbing?*

Dressing true to yourself—while bowing to circumstance Big-city woman . . . small-town client • You're a kooky-lover • Dinner with the boss • Natural-born whistle bait • He wants you satiny-sexy.

Changing your image in transition times

husband do you have? • What can you expect? • Can this be love?

Think ahead coping techniques Basic survival kits • Master records • Date doings • Bulk buying • Lifesavers • Shortcuts • Smart timing

LOOKING,
WORKING,
LIVING
TERRIFIC
24 HOURS
A DAY

BEING THE BEST YOU CAN BE

If you're one of today's working women, trying to juggle the demands of a promising career, a pell-mell private life (with or without husband and children) and an unwavering insistence on personal style—this book is for you.

If you feel you have a right to aim for all that and to achieve it—without being Superwoman—this book is especially for you.

When I started the field of Image Consulting eleven years ago, my main aim was to help my clients present to the world the best image of themselves. Because I knew that if I could help them get their image together, it would be the fastest, most direct route to help them feel better about themselves.

I had no inkling at the time how much more far-reaching the effects would be. Only after helping hundreds of women with my service and reading the letters from all over the country in response to my first book, *Looking Terrific*, did I come to realize the bigger social significance of getting one's image into focus.

Very simply, it tells the world that *you're* in focus. And the world reacts accordingly. People look on you with interest, admiration, trust, respect. You, in turn, react as any human being does when treated as an important person—you become more interesting, admirable, trustable, worthy of respect. Even if you aren't quite there to start with, if your image says you are, the world expects the best of you—and you live up to it. The result? Developing an authentic personal image—one you're comfortable with, one that makes the most of your unique individuality—miraculously helps you get your entire life in order.

There's no high quite like it. When your image reflects your best you, you beam the message that you're on top of your life, and doing fine. Yet too many women never experience that high, never get a chance to feel that good about themselves, what they're doing, and how they're doing it. Because today's woman is trying to do more, live more, *be* more than any woman in history.

That's why I wanted to write this second book—to offer special help to the woman who works, takes care of a family, runs a house, and on top of it all, still has the pressure of looking her best, and through her style, identifying herself. It's women like her—the jugglers—I have the most empathy for. Perhaps because I'm one too.

I know how it feels to want to be the best you can be, in every aspect of your life. You want to grow in your job, to have an effect on the people you deal with and the work you turn out. You want to make a crucial difference in the lives of those you love. You always want to be there when it counts—there for the attention they need from a mother, the encouragement he needs from a wife, the support they need from a daughter, the understanding they need from a friend. You want to develop your personal style, a style that will give your world a lift in the way you look and dress, in the skills with which you handle your personal relationships, and in the open pride you show in the way you present yourself.

I also know how it feels when you think you're not up to it or, worse still, when you think that you never will be up to it, that only Superwoman can do it—and you're not Superwoman.

We all feel that way sometimes. But the fact is—as I've learned from my own experience and that of my clients—you're a lot more "super" than you think. It doesn't take special talent, special drive. All it takes is two things, both grounded in personal style: using the art of clothing to send out the best message about yourself to get the right responses, and changing the way *you* do things to make them simpler, faster, easier, and more rewarding.

How to get from *frenzy to focus* is what this book is all about. From my work as an image consultant for over eleven years, and from my clients, many of whom I have interviewed for their solutions, I've learned a great deal about how to be a working woman/wife/ mother—with all the overload that entails—and *feel good about yourself.* And that's what I'd like to share with you. You start by finding your image, which is the springboard to putting yourself in control of your life—Looking, Working, Living Terrific 24 Hours a Day.

EMILY CHO

1

THE PROBLEM:
Is This Your Life?

You open an eye. The clock can't be saying what it's saying. Bill's away and you've overslept and today's the day you have a client presentation. How's that for openers?

Out of the bed into the shower, out of the shower and into the second crisis of the day. What are you going to wear to make that wonderful impression on that important new client?

Radio says rain, maybe. Sky says ditto. A cold, client day calls for something warm—and executive. Your gray suit, of course. Blouse? Your favorite blouse is at the cleaners. You have your pick of the classic white silk (no pizzazz), the pink bow blouse (too sweet), the striped cotton (too workaday), the blue turtleneck sweater (too chummy). Well—um-m-m—there's the green silk print. (Can't take a chance—green's unlucky. Besides, you're feeling a little green yourself today.)

Oh all right, the white silk—at least it's safe.

Pantyhose . . . are you really down to three pairs? First pair: has a run you didn't notice before. So wear boots and who's to know? Strike boots—they're at the shoemaker with a stuck zipper. Second pair: the last of the size A you can't get into since you put 5 pounds on your hips over the holidays. Third pair: taupe. Not quite the color for your luggage brown shoes. The maroon shoes then? Heels too low for the suit—make you feel low on the totem pole. Your black patent pumps? Won't quite go with the tan shoulder bag. Back to square one—taupe pantyhose. And keep your feet under the desk all day.

Time's a-wasting. Let's get *dressed.* No time for makeup—put it on at the office. Hair: total disaster, three weeks overdue for a cut, and it looks hopelessly slept-on. Emergency blow-dry repair blows fifteen minutes. Into your skirt, on with the blouse and—damn!—the middle button is missing. Can't change now. So keep your suit jacket buttoned. No time for coffee, much less breakfast. No time to make the bed, do leftover dishes. Who expected to be stuck at the office till 10 P.M.? And by the time you got home, sleep got the nod over shiny clean dishes.

You're lucky at last—there's a cab at the corner. When you arrive at the office, the rain's turned serious. You dash across 30 feet of plaza in your open-toed, slingback shoes without hitting a puddle. But your stockings are still polka-dotted with mud spots.

At least it's so late there won't be anybody you know on the elevator. And you're half right. There are only two other people—one of whom is the head of your department.

You scuttle into the ladies room to put on your makeup. You remembered everything except the moisturizer and the eyelash curler. Who's going to notice that your eyes look smaller and that you're makeup's not on evenly? You wash the polka dots off your stockings and figure you'll pick up a pair of pantyhose at the all-purpose newsstand in the lobby at lunch.

And so you do. But all they carry is a brand you've never tried before—"one size fits all." It turns out it may fit all—but not you. The leg part is so long you've got wrinkled ankles. You put your wrong-colored taupe pantyhose back on.

You put on your presentation in the afternoon at the client meeting, and it seems to go quite well. You feel a little awkward handling the flip charts because you can't move in your carefully buttoned suit jacket, but at least nobody knows you're missing a button, and nobody can see how hot and sticky your blouse is by the end of the meeting.

At a quarter to five you get a call from your husband, just back from his business trip, having run into an old college buddy he hasn't seen in ten years on the plane. Bill wants to take him to dinner at the poshest restaurant in town, and he'll pick you up at 5:30 for drinks. There's no time to go home to change, and you can't face the poshest restaurant in town in your sticky wrinkled blouse and your Old Faithful gray suit. Bill's a little dashed when you suggest going to the little hideaway around the corner instead—but he's very sweet about it. Not exactly understanding, but sweet.

He is sweet also about the sinkful of dishes when you get home. He doesn't even mention them. You make the bed before you both fall into it. Bill plummets into sleep. And you review the day.

You felt behind before you even got up . . . you felt off-balance, uncertain, *inadequate* all day, and though you put on a good presentation, you felt more like a loser than a winner.

Yet you're one of the up-and-coming ones. Your boss says so . . . your husband says so . . . your record says so. You even know it yourself. You know you've got what it takes—but somehow it just doesn't seem to show. You don't look like it . . . you don't act like it . . . worst of all, you don't *feel* like it.

And you've got lots of company.

Not every day of every working woman is a replica of the log above. Anybody can have a bad day on occasion. It's the cumulative effect of too many ordinary things going wrong on too many ordinary days that saps self-esteem.

But you don't have to let it happen to you—as I know from the clients I've worked with. Over the years I've seen firsthand how they cope with the demands and frustrations of the full lives they lead. And what a difference it makes when we help them get their clothing image right—for their particular body, their particular personality, and their day-to-day life.

When you're a working woman, the principles that make for living well are not all that different from those for dressing well. To dress well, you should know who you are . . . where you're going. Your wardrobe should cover your interests and activities in all their variety. Your clothes should give you cheer and enjoyment and freedom. You should be able to depend on them as much as you delight in them. They shouldn't be part of the problem, they should be part of the solution.

At this point, especially if you've had a bad day, you may be thinking, "That all sounds nice, but you can't get there from here."

Yes, you can. I'll share with you how the many women I've interviewed say they've done it.

In the chapters ahead, you'll see how your working life—and your private life—can be noticeably eased and enhanced as theirs have been, when you evolve the right clothing image and put it to work for you.

As one friend told me, "It's like the difference between just not being sick and discovering what it's like to be wildly healthy! You know, you live for years at what you think is OK health—even though you know there's too much junk food, not enough exercise. And then one day you decide to reform—you're into salads and milk and jogging and plenty of sleep. And in a matter of months, you're a different person, a dynamo! That's what learning to dress right has done for me."

2

MAKING IT—
Beyond Superwoman

Before you take that first step toward your new image . . . before you look in the mirror . . . look around. Look at the era we're in now: the new living patterns . . . the new standards of style and beauty and performance . . . the new goals we're setting for ourselves. They all have a bearing on the image you evolve for yourself.

Ten years ago only forty percent of my clients were working. Today it's more like ninety percent. Already the two-paycheck family is the norm, instead of the trendy minority. Year by year, competition gets stiffer—yet month by month it's harder to avoid. Indeed, for most of us, it's not a matter of choice. We *have* to work. If we're single—we work for personal fulfillment as well as a paycheck. If we're married—we realize that two can get ahead faster than one to reach those dreams we share. If we're single parents—we work to stay afloat and keep a sturdy life raft under our children. If we're middle or late-life returnees—we enter the work world to renew our energy and spirit and keep ourselves young at any age.

But as any working woman knows—or soon finds out—a woman who works always has *two* jobs. The one she gets paid for and the one she's born with—the job of *being a woman*. These days, having one doesn't let you off the hook for having the other. The world

25

expects us to be good at both and what's more important, we expect it of ourselves.

Yet our time is limited, our standards are higher, our hopes and goals are escalating, help is disappearing—something, you will say, has *got* to give. I'm here to say it doesn't have to be You. Rather, it's old notions, conventional expectations, worn-out ways of doing things, irrelevant standards of excellence—they're what have to give. And *you* have to be the one who makes them.

The changes are happening all around you—and it's women like you who are making them happen. Perhaps they're easiest to see in the area of style and fashion . . . in what we now call beautiful . . , and, most especially, in how we women are thinking about ourselves, as I learned over and over again from the interviews I had with my clients.

What's different? Fashion, still that iron hand in velvet glove, is losing its grip on us. We don't salute every time it sends up a new flag. But that doesn't mean we forget about dress entirely. More and more of us are joining the work force, and work still has its dress codes—even though we're right to refuse to get into "uniform." How to reflect the professional code with individuality is the new challenge we have to meet—and beat—today. (And that's what this book will attempt to do in detail.)

Our notions of beauty, too, are changing. In this new age, beauty is energy. No longer is beauty confined to a Raquel Welch curve or a Bo Derek profile . . . limited to the very few lucky ones among us. No longer do we achieve beauty by "hiding" our faults and imperfections—under a Farah Fawcett hairdo, Hollywood makeup, body-binding clothes. I tell my clients it's character that counts today—character that draws people's attention, holds their interest. Even the models in the magazines are no longer the look-alike, paper-doll pretties of a few years ago. For us now, beauty is the exciting mix of energy and individuality.

But the most significant change of all is in our attitude about ourselves. We may not know exactly where our lives are going, but we know where we've been and we're not going to settle for it. We won't go back to being everybody's Mommy as in the '50s. And we won't be pressured into being Superwoman. She's an idea whose time has come . . . and gone. Superwoman—the one who has it all, does it all, manages it all so well and so completely—too often has no quiet time to enjoy and to savor her supercharged life. It's summed up in the one plaint I've heard over and over again in one form or another from my friends and clients: "What really bothers me is, I'm so busy keeping on top of the situation, I can't really experience the *moment*."

Perhaps the most basic mistake we working women make—and given our frenetic lives, it's so easy to make—is to assume unconsciously that "keeping on top of the situation" is the goal. It isn't. It's the means to the goal—which is living your life, not just surviving it. That's what this book is about.

In the pages ahead, I'll show you how the most surprising changes in the way you look, the confidence you feel, the impression you make on the people around you, and even the style with which you handle your job, will come from such a simple starting place as choosing the right clothes that define your image. Your true—and best—self.

3

YOUR IMAGE:
The Real You?
The Non-You?
The Best You?

There's a lot of talk these days about "image." How important your image is . . . how it can help you or hurt you . . . what you should or shouldn't do about it.

Some people are uncomfortable with the very word itself. To them, it means sham or cover-up—an attempt to hide the real self, especially flaws. Others think creating an image is a shortcut to success. They believe that if you have the "right image" you hardly need anything else, including competence, knowledge, background, honesty, talent. For me, "image" is a true reflection of you—as true as your image in the mirror. At the same time, creating the right image is a marvelous way to help you become your best self.

I learned very quickly from my clients, most of whom work, that the way they dressed was not a true reflection of who they were or even what they felt themselves to be. Again and again, as I got to know them, I was struck by how unaware they were that they were sending messages at all—much less accurate messages about themselves. All they sensed was a certain nagging, uncomfortable feeling that they could and should look better.

Developing a true image of your best self, as only you know her, is what dressing well is all about. It's especially important if you're a working woman with high ambitions and a realistic appraisal of the competition all around you. If you change your clothing image, over time *you'll* change. You'll become more sure of yourself, more outgoing because of that, and therefore more relaxed. You'll have more energy on the job and off the job, because you won't be wasting energy worrying about how you look and whether you measure up. And the happiest change of all will be in how good you feel about yourself. For the first time, you won't be working against yourself and your aims. You and the way you present yourself will be one and the same.

Not really. No matter what you wear, you're always naked in a sense, because your clothes are always sending messages about you. They telegraph your economic class, your educational level, your social position, your level of sophistication, your trustworthiness, your hopes, your fears, your savvy (or lack of it), your state of mind, and your *joie de vivre*.

Do clothes ever lie?

People don't have to know about your private life if you don't want them to, but they'll read everything about you—right or not—from the way you dress, since they have no other information to go on. Their response will come from feeling they have read you accurately. So you can only do yourself a favor by communicating your image message clearly.

Some people feel you shouldn't care what others think of your image, but that's unrealistic. People pass judgment on the basis of superficial impressions. If your look is dull and dreary, you may be easily bypassed because of the impression you're giving. If you don't feel good and sure about yourself, it shows in many ways. You don't project the confidence you'd like to project. You're not as spontaneous as you wish you were. You're shyer, more reluctant to reach out to people. You retire into the corner, not using the opportunity when it presents itself. You purposely don't remember why you are

Should you care?

attending the event in the first place. Worse yet, you refuse even to go—and play the game.

So clothes, when you come right down to it, are not superficial at all. Indeed, we don't give clothes credit for the power they have. And therefore, we never fully utilize them for our own benefit.

Super-talented people may begin, and remain, eccentric—but there aren't many of them. For the rest of us, clothes should help us in our climb. After all, few things about us attract as much attention or immediate approval as our clothes.

Breaking into the winner's circle

Over and over again, research studies and psychological experiments have shown that both men and women judge attractive people as more skilled, brighter intellectually, and more socially likable. (Proving yet again the truth of that old saying, "Them that has, gets.")

If you change the impression your clothes make, you'll set off a whole series of changes in people's responses to you. When people respond differently, how *you* feel about yourself will change. And before you know it, there you are in the winner's circle, where things keep getting better and better.

Your image can be a wonderful, magical tool to open doors for you, to help get you where you want to go.

If on the other hand you stop caring about how you look, you'll lose that delight in living that people are instinctively attracted to. Being poorly dressed over time leads to a chronic feeling of inferiority and inadequacy, especially for a woman.

Is your body getting in the way?

It's hard to sort out your feelings about your body and your clothes. How you judge one affects how you feel about the other. The worst obstacle is to be so self-conscious about your body that it overshadows your personality. You're not happy, and others don't know—or care—why.

Almost every woman—no matter how beautiful she may be—is insecure about some aspect of her body. When a man slips on his jacket, he seems able to forget about his physique underneath. The cut and quality of his clothes take over and become his self-image.

But when a woman slips on her dress it is as if it were transparent. She never forgets her body underneath—her lumpy arms or her good bosom or her large thighs. Clothes, for her, are closely tied in to her body image. Because society has tied them together, to her they have become the same.

We women try so hard to look beautiful. If we don't succeed as much as we would like, it's not because we don't try hard enough. It's because we don't try in the right places . . . the right ways. We concentrate on losing those stubborn 5 pounds we think are ruining our figures or trimming the extra half-inch around our hips. We bemoan our "heavy bones" or our hair that is only just hair-color, neither dazzling blond nor ravishing brunette. We constantly bad-mouth ourselves to ourselves.

Beauty is not as far out of reach as we think—if we'd just approach it from a different angle. People don't look at us with a disdainful eye fixed on that extra half-inch, those extra 5 pounds. They look at the whole person in front of them, and what they see is something we can do a lot more about, in a lot less time, than trimming half an inch, or losing 5 pounds.

What they see is how we carry ourselves, how straight we stand, how gracefully we move, how alive our faces are. How our clothes suit us, flatter us, attract people to us. In sum, people sense how happy we are just being who we are. And they respond accordingly.

The secret is to make yourself aware of yourself as you enter a room or rise from a chair. Take a moment to collect yourself. Rise to your full height before you start walking forward. The minute you straighten up, hold yourself proudly, move gracefully; you'll be surprised at the improvement. The trick is to make yourself remember to do it.

In your head—and in your muscles—try to keep a sense of young movement to improve your walk. It's not your bones that are "heavy"—they're only one-fifth of your body weight. Instead of coming down hard on your heels, cultivate a light quick step. And wear the kind of shoes that will let you do it—shoes that fit just right, with a heel that won't have you mincing or clomping.

These are the things that add up to a very special kind of beauty. The beauty that makes you one of a kind. It's not a beauty given at birth, but beauty *achieved*. You can take credit for this kind of beauty and *that* builds a self-confidence nothing can take away from you.

When you like yourself enough to do everything you do with the same consistency of image—whether it's wrapping a present so distinctively friends know it's from you before they open it, or giving a memorable party, or running a complicated project with unflappable skill—that's panache, a personal asset that outscores mere prettiness every time.

Can clothes matter too much?

One reason many of us can't decide what role clothes should play in our lives is what we were taught as children: that clothes shouldn't be too important to us because, if they were, people wouldn't take us seriously. When we grow up to become doctors or lawyers or business executives, we feel the pressure even more. No hint of being a sex object can be allowed to undermine our image as a savvy professional. Once we've established our credentials and our reputation, it's safe—indeed, it's wise—to let our clothes celebrate the fact that we are, after all, female and all the more special for it. As one fashion authority puts it, "A woman should maintain the fact that she's a woman, and that she's succeeding as a woman." Most of the women I know want to do just that.

One way or another, your clothes are going to make an impression. Why should you allow that impression to arise incidentally? It makes much more sense to *create* the impression you want and escape mistakes and misrepresentation.

An interior designer friend once told me that she had discovered the clothes she wore determined whether her clients would be muddled or decisive about an expensive high-style sofa she was recommending. If her outfit was mediocre, her client would be wishy-washy, and her job of finding the ideal sofa would drag on because the client subconsciously didn't trust her judgment.

Clothes are silent persuaders. They give people reason to have faith in your skill and competence. In the same way, clothes show the hierarchy of power: who is stronger, more powerful, more sure.

Clothes also show that your inner self counts more than your outer measurements, as designer Bob Mackie can attest to. Two of his most famous clients—Cher and Carol Burnett—had exactly the same measurements, yet neither could wear the other's clothes . . . clothes he had designed for them. They were entirely different types, and each one's clothes reflected her own person.

32

When I see the delicate interplay between clothes and personality work—and succeed—for my clients, it's the most deeply satisfying and enjoyable part of my work. Each year, as their clothing image is clarified and refined, their personalities seem to change accordingly, and they become more confident and easy with who they are. Image is an uncanny barometer.

Today, working women—however different their tastes and preferences—all seem to be asking for the same thing. They all want a professional pulled-together image that wins respect yet lets them feel comfortable. Some may lean toward femininity, others focus on neatness. Some care most about comfort or freedom from upkeep. Others want more individuality in textures and colors, and, to get what they want, are willing to take on the extra cleaning and pressing entailed.

But all my clients come with one conviction: If they can get their image together, the most valuable by-product (guaranteed!) is self-esteem. And that new confidence will free them to concentrate their energy on job performance, instead of frittering it away on their imagined shortcomings.

One client, a top executive, uses clothes to set the level of taste for the whole organization she runs and to underline the fact that *she's* the boss. Off-duty, she wears wild fantasy clothes, to achieve other important aims: to split work from private life, to prove she's a fun-loving type, and that it's OK to relax.

How different women use their image

Another friend is a very savvy woman in her sixties who works on TV, a field that rarely has use for anyone over thirty-five. She spends a lot of time on her image and turns herself out each day so smartly, her bosses can't fail to get the message she's in full control. Always in pretty colors or an interesting blend of textures, she comes off not only looking her best, but young and energetic to boot. Clothing is her tool and has become her edge.

If you're shy and always too tongue-tied to make the first move, choose the right image and your clothes can do it for you. Clothes that enhance, flatter, and attract can say what you can't and make up for your initial shyness. In the same way, if you have a speech to give or a meeting to preside over, and you're afraid you may revert to an earlier, less-sure self, dress in a powerful outfit of quality and it won't happen. Your image will help keep you in command.

Who do you think you are? (Or don't you know?)   A woman who knows who she is presents a consistent image to the world, no matter how varied are the roles she plays and the moods she expresses. If you're not at that point, your clothes may reflect your conflicts and inconsistencies. You surprise people in ways they don't understand, which makes them uncertain and, therefore, wary. If, for instance, you show up in a sophisticated gabardine suit and wild purple cowboy boots, they don't know which part of the inconsistency is the basic you and which is the aberration. So they may size you up wrong. Or, if they're not sure how to size you up, they may just turn away rather than make a mistake.

Intriguing or disturbing?   If you lack image integrity, it means some striking aspect of your presentation is out of sync with who you are. If the striking aspect is a plus, people can be intrigued and attracted, and may give you the benefit of the doubt, at least for a little while, in regard to the "minus" they also see. If, for instance, you're definitely Park Avenue chic—but your accent is unmistakably Brooklyn—you'll attract people on first acquaintance, but your goal should be to improve your speech to the level of your taste, so that the initial favorable impression will not fade because people are disturbed or puzzled by the contradiction you face them with.

Many women make a common mistake: It doesn't seem to occur to them to take care to change their private-life image when they first take on a new job. For instance, the sexy lady who comes to work in sheer, plunging-neckline blouses sends the message that it isn't work she's after, it's a man. Or the disheveled type who always looks sloppy and uncoordinated tells the world, "I don't feel too good about myself." The fragile, frail girl in pale ruffles and soft voice says, "I need protection. Treat me with kid gloves or I won't be able to take it." The funky dresser who changes from glitter jewelry to jodhpurs gives the message, "I'm not reliable. I won't be around long."

34

DRESSING TRUE TO YOURSELF—
WHILE BOWING TO CIRCUMSTANCE

There'll be times in business—and in your private life as well—when your position and surroundings will be quite different from the kind of person you are. How, then, should you dress? As the person you are—even if it makes you look quite out of place? Or as the occasion demands—even though you won't feel like you? This is one of the trickiest problems a woman faces in learning how to dress well. Not only because it comes up again and again, but because so much rides on how successfully she does it.

No matter what the situation, if you don't dress true to yourself, you're going to feel uncomfortable. You won't feel natural, honest, or relaxed. And when you're ill-at-ease, everyone else will be too.

On the other hand, if you don't take the circumstances into consideration, you're going to make the people you deal with uncomfortable. They'll feel you've distanced yourself . . . that you think you're better than they are . . . that you don't give much weight to their standards or customs or taste. In a word, that you either don't care, or you're not very bright. Probably both. And again, the unease will be catching.

It is not a cop-out to adjust your outfit to the situation. It's a kindness and a courtesy. The whole point of dressing well is that it makes everybody feel better. All it takes is a little thought and empathy.

Say you're a big-city woman doing business with a small-town client. For important meetings in the city you usually appear in your cream gabardine suit. Your client owns the family business and gets out of town at most three or four times a year. The nearest thing to a female executive in his town is probably the president of the League of Women Voters. Do you wear your cream wool suit or a pretty blue dress? Your pretty blue dress.

Big-city woman . . .
small-town client

35

You're a kooky-lover   You really love clothes with a certain kooky individuality—but you have an interview with a large accounting firm. Do you wear your long tweed midi-skirt with your black embroidered jacket? Or your regular-length striped wool skirt with your teal blue velvet blazer? You wear your regular-length skirt and velvet blazer.

Dinner with the boss   You're having dinner with the boss—and his very threatened wife. Should you wear your peach ruffle-neck dinner dress—or your tailored gray silk two-piece dress? You wear your tailored gray silk two-piece dress.

Natural-born whistle bait   You're natural-born whistle-bait, but you don't like whistles. You jog in a sports-bra and loose jogging suit—not in short-shorts and a T-shirt.

He wants you satiny-sexy   Your husband wants you satiny-sexy—but you've got a blue-jeans soul. Perhaps he's detected a streak of sex and satin you didn't know you had. Perhaps he's righter about it than you. Experiment in your private life with luscious lingerie, beautiful loungewear, etc. All in easy stages. (You don't have to go from plaid flannel bathrobes to marabou and satin in one dizzying jump.) See how it feels to swap your white cotton briefs for a silky, lace-lavished teddy in blue. Changes out of the public eye are often easier to make—and take. A few little changes get you ready to take the big ones in stride.

CHANGING YOUR IMAGE IN TRANSITION TIMES

The most difficult time to shape our clothing image is during transitional times in our lives. In college, for instance, peer pressure keeps people from dressing better. Wear anything fancier than jeans and a sweater, and you're instantly rejected. After adjusting to that, it's definite culture shock to change to high heels and a tailored suit when you're trying to break into the business world.

36

One word of caution. If you're not quite up to the level you're aiming for in your company, it's not only permissible, it's often smart to reach a little in your image—to dress as if you were already on the next rung up. But you must be subtle. Nothing annoys others more than a person who "jumps the gun," suddenly dressing two levels above where they are themselves. The secretary who just inherited money from a rich aunt is suddenly no longer one of the gang when she jumps to designer clothes. Your competition doesn't like it if you haven't put your time in, as they've had to. The only legitimate way you can claim an image as your own is to cultivate and refine it slowly.

The fact is, it's wise not to change your image too fast in any aspect of your life. Consider your husband or lover, employer, parents, children—people who have definite ideas about who you are and what they expect you to look like. You don't want to deprive them, overnight, of the person they've known so long. But you have to grow and change in your own way. You may surprise your near and dear ones as you begin getting your look together. Don't shock them by changing totally at once. Gradual change will probably be better for you—and better for them—because you can integrate it more. On the other hand, it's not necessary to get *everybody's* approval. It's your life, your body, your future.

4

YOUR JOB:
Getting There—With Style

You may feel there are two kinds of women in the world—those who were born with a natural talent for dressing well and those who weren't. You may then assume that any woman in the first category will instinctively know how to dress right for her job, and any woman in the second category will not.

And you might just be wrong on all counts.

First off, there's more to dressing right on the job than just having a sense of what's right for *you*. There's more to consider than just the color of your complexion or the shape of your body or the kind of personality you have. As important as these aspects of dressing—possibly even more important sometimes—are considerations like the kind of company you work for, the kind of people you work with, the kind of work you do; where you're pegged on the organization chart, and where you aim to go; whether it's smart to look your age or not. And a hundred other things this chapter is all about.

And if you think you're one of those who weren't born with a natural talent for dressing well, think again. *It's not a natural talent.* It's a learnable skill. Just like your job. You can learn the basics . . . practice the principles . . . make a mistake now and then. And one day, sooner than you think, you've got the hang of it. You know you can do it. And it shows. If you're smart enough to do the job, you're smart enough to dress right for it.

DECODING THE DRESS CODE

On the office grapevine, clothes speak louder than words. Do you know what message you're sending? Your clothing could classify you before anyone gets to know you or your capabilities. And that first impression stays with people a long time.

If you arrive the first day in a red dress, the message is loud and clear. "Not only am I very much here, but I want everyone to know it—and fast." There's a lot of confidence built into a red dress—but it can be a two-edged sword. If you've already got the confidence, you can live up to the message the dress is sending. But why set up standards you have to meet so early in the game? Especially when you don't have to. If, on the other hand, you're wearing red hoping it will give you confidence, you're setting up future problems for yourself that are unnecessary.

An advertising executive I know told me about her first interviews at the agency. Since the weather was rainy and dismal, she ran out and bought a chic white vinyl raincoat at the most fashionable shop she knew. The coat was most appropriate since she was being interviewed for a fashion job, and the agency was very "with it." She wore the coat to both her interviews, got the job, and became a real success at the agency. Ten years later, her account supervisor still refers to her as "the spy in the white vinyl trenchcoat." See the importance of that first impression?

A capable young woman working for a textile company was almost done in by her liking for smock dresses. She looked young to begin with, and smock dresses took another five years off her age. When her coworkers began to be promoted and she wasn't—though she was excellent at her job—she went to her supervisor to find out why. During the conversation she learned that her supervisor had thought she was much younger than she was. Her clothes had almost hurt her chances for a well-earned promotion.

In another instance, a top retail chain was interviewing their own

39

employees for the executive training program, the only way to break into management at this firm. Ellen, a very bright young woman, wanted desperately to qualify for the program. Luckily she had a friend in management who stepped in with some wise advice before the scheduled interview. Ellen is 5'4". Her hair (her pride and joy) was waist-length. She usually dressed in folkloric clothing with brightly colored opaque stockings—right for selling in this with-it store, but not for a management job.

Her friend explained that management would be looking for leadership potential in the interview and her excellent record would not be enough. First, she recommended that Ellen tie her hair back and knot it loosely at the nape of her neck. Ellen then wore the one silk dress in her closet—red and taupe stripe—with neutral taupe stockings and taupe shoes. The transformation was startling. Not only did it get Ellen into the program, but it proved she had two looks, equally good for her. From then on she used them both in appropriate circumstances. *Looking right for the part can get you the job.*

The "New Uniform"

The new, sophisticated, working woman's "uniform." It's not a navy blue suit. We're ready for more. Molloy is wrong in *Dress for Success.* In recent years, when women started entering the work force in noticeable numbers and had to compete with men, they assumed the fastest way to become "equal" was to wear a suit. And tone down their makeup. And carry a briefcase, needed or not.

That's over—to a great extent. With the exception of banking (and even that business has softened), women can be women again. And a good thing too. Because women have found the dress-for-success formula has its problems. Aside from emotional rigidity and terminal boredom, the basic problem is figure. Suits just don't work for every figure.

A woman who is very heavy just can't buy one off the rack, and can't afford to have more than one or two made to order. Another who has a totally disproportionate top and bottom finds it impossible to buy the same size top and bottom in one suit. Or the jacket is cut too long or the skirt too short. These are "abnormal" figures—if you define anything not quite perfect as abnormal. The new sophisticated working woman's uniform arises out of necessity, practicality, and budget considerations, to say nothing of individuality, ease and comfort—and a fight against the old rigidity.

You don't have time to look for a suit that doesn't exist for you. If you can wear only sweater jackets and skirts to camouflage your particular problem (if, for instance, you're too wide in the shoulder to wear a fitted jacket comfortably), then that's what you should wear. If you're so short a suit makes you all but disappear, if you've tried the new petite lines and they don't work—there's nothing wrong with a smart dress. You want to look *your* very best.

If a "uniform" is a look you've created for yourself that expresses your style and comfort, that's fine. If it's a calculated masculine-looking way to keep up with the competition, then it's passé. Women have earned the right to relax into their femininity.

What's most intriguing to others—and most fun for yourself—is when you've reached the stage where you are always changing the different pieces and parts of your wardrobe, from suits to skirts and blouses, from sweater jackets topped with shawls to wool two-piece flared dresses or silk sheaths. At this highly evolved stage, you manage to keep up interest, maintain a certain standard of a finished outfit, and always define the clear image of who you are and what

The "Old Uniform"—
the classic "safe" suit that isn't—
because it sinks you into the crowd
and makes no individual statement.

41

The *"New Uniform"*—
4 right ways to say
"all business"—
4 bright ways to say "all me"—
professional, yet
creative and individual.

you want others to feel about you. Dressing well is like a beautiful piece of music—a symphony made up of related but contrasting movements that can always be identified by the underlying theme of the whole.

Today, "all business" can be expressed in a creative, professional look as you can see by four varied examples of the "new uniform" illustrated on pages 42–43. Plunging necklines and super-clingy knit dresses will never be appropriate, but a knit suit with structure—a Chanel knit, say—can have a marvelously chic look. Individuality can be allowed to surface. Keep your strict suit for that serious board meeting, and wear a soft turtleneck dress for a day when you can relax, have no important meetings, or are going out casually after work. On a high-action day, when you know you'll feel too constricted in a jacket, wear your beautiful rose blouse with a matching skirt, and let smart gold accessories pull your look together. Then when you do put on the suit, it will just have all the more impact.

You don't have to be "two-suit" Mary—or worse, "wrong-suit" Mary. More and more men are willing to admit that women can be their equals professionally and still look like attractive women, not junior men.

How to look like the pros, even when you're a cub

Pros know more. And it shows. It shows in quality—quality of their work, quality of their taste, quality of their clothes. It doesn't always have to do with a difference in age. More than the years you've had, it's your interest in learning how to tell the first-rate from the mediocre . . . learning it so well it becomes second nature.

Women with a true love of clothes pick it up early. And people recognize that talent they've acquired even when they can't put a name to it. Quality shows—and tells. And confers more stature on a person who insists on it.

Inexpensive clothes chosen with flair and taste can do great things for you, but for asserting your sophistication, competence, and good judgment (your claim to be taken as a professional), nothing takes the place of quality. Take two beige suits that look almost the same in cut, fabric, color—you'll still be able to sense which is the better quality, even when you can't explain it.

Quality is the sum total of care and concern in a hundred little details, and it's worth every penny you spend for it. Because, more often than you think, your supervisors will translate the quality you show in your clothes into the quality they can expect in your work. For the specifics on quality, see page 94.

DRESSING FOR TWO—YOUR COMPANY AND YOU

What's your company's style? Rock-bottom conservative? Way out . . . anything goes? Middle-of-the-road conventional? It shouldn't take long to size up the corporate image and take your cue accordingly. While there's been a welcome loosening up of company rules in recent years, anyone who differs too strongly from the norm at a particular company is going to feel a little uncomfortable a good part of the time and make others feel that way too.

Not everyone who works in a bank needs to be in a pin-striped three-piece suit, but if you show up more than once in a blue velour jumpsuit or a gypsy skirt with a halter top, people are going to wonder just how seriously you take banking as a career. Especially your boss. If, on the other hand, you work for a Broadway agent who specializes in punk rock groups, you're not going to telegraph the expected dazzle sitting behind the desk in a proper white shirt and neat navy skirt.

Most people gravitate toward companies they feel at home with—and a good thing too. But if your finances force you to take a job with a company whose soul is not yours and whose dress codes aren't either, what do you do? Bend a little so you won't look too stubborn. If everybody's wearing tailored suits and you would live in prairie skirts with petticoats if you could, show up in the professional version of that look: a dark wool flared midi-skirt without a ruffle. They'll appreciate the effort you made to see the good in their way.

Companies that fall into the classification rock-bottom conservative are fewer than they used to be, but they still exist. They include banks across the board, some law firms, some Wall Street firms, some corporations. These businesses will be happiest to see you in matched suits in very conservative colors like navy, gray, brown, and taupe. Blazers and tweed skirts with conservative blouses. Constructed suits and constructed dresses in quiet or dark colors and prints.

Firms and professions of conservative cast are even more strict about what they don't like. If you had to sum up their stand in one sentence, it would be: "Don't wear anything that calls attention away from the work at hand to the person involved—meaning you." This is why you won't see a smart woman lawyer wearing chartreuse silk before a judge . . . or a woman treasurer wearing a pants suit at a board meeting . . . or a woman loan officer in a tight red sweater.

Whatever your job is, if your company is conservative, these are the specific "nos" to avoid:

No plunging necklines	No see-through fabrics
No cling	No glittery fabrics
No loud colors	No pants
No very short skirts	No tight skirts
No sweaters	No tight anything

The rank of companies where "anything goes" has also thinned since the '60s and '70s, but they're still very much alive in certain fields, especially those connected with show business and the arts. Among them you'll find some ad agencies (mostly the small brash ones), some cosmetic firms, boutiques, P.R. firms, a few fashion and beauty magazines, some garment center businesses, some companies in the music business, movies, and theater.

For these mavericks, there are no "nos." Everything goes—from knickers to gold lamé jumpsuits. Safari looks, cowboy boots, lots of makeup, lots of hair, the newest in zany accessories. The more fun and kicky the look, the more you'll see of it.

Still in the middle of the road are the companies that make up most of American business, from the great conglomerates to the small-town five and ten. In the middle is where you'll find most law firms and brokerage houses, most ad agencies and P.R. firms, most insurance companies and corporations. Grade schools, high schools, colleges, libraries, government offices. Also some retail fashion stores, boutiques, newspapers, garment center firms.

What goes with all these is a more casual variation of the conservative look. Nonmatched suits, relaxed jackets, sweater jackets, tailored gabardine pants, appropriate sweaters, a variety of dresses, interesting accessories—open to your own interpretation of what's chic and fashionable and flattering on you.

46

If you love bright colors, it's not easy to give them up during your working week. Yet your choice of color on the job says more about your level of taste and sophistication—and your place in the business world—than you might think.

Handling color— with flying colors

You can prove this to yourself just by looking at the women around you, both below and above you, and seeing how they handle color. You won't find many women executives in kelly green or shocking pink. Or, in fact, intense anything. But if you think they spend their working day in dull, mousy, boring colors that fade off into the woodwork, look again. You'll see that the beiges, grays, dusty "off" shades they choose are not dull, but subtle. Not mousy, but quietly authoritative; not boring, but intriguing. And look at their mix of textures.

When you look at the listing below, make sure the basics of your wardrobe are in the colors of Column 1. You can add the variety and color you want by choosing blouses, scarves, and accessories in colors from Column 2. And if you can't bear to do without the brash colors in Column 3, save them for your play life or private life.

OFFICE COLORS/TEXTURES, PATTERNS

Always Safe		Sometimes Safe	Chancy
Brown	Muted red	Fuchsia	Shocking pink
Beige	Cream (on top)	Gold	Kelly green
Gray	White (on top)	Muted turquoise	Intense aqua
Black	Dusty and "off"	Lavender	Sunflower yellow
Navy	colors:	Muted pink	Chartreuse
Burgundy	Bottle green	Soft pink	Screaming orange
Camel	Olive	Soft blue	
Rust	Mauve	Soft yellow	
Any subtle	Taupe	Tomato red	
shade of a	Teal blue	Pale green	
primary color			
Pinstripes		Bold stripes	Very bulky fabrics
Quiet tweeds		Multicolored	Very sheer fabrics
Small plaids		tweeds	Lots of lace
Small floral patterns		Large plaids	
		Large floral patterns	
		Some lace trim	

The following charts show all the various looks possible from just a few right pieces in a wardrobe. (Third layers of jackets and shawl, in parentheses, are optional.) Learn to recognize the principles involved in making a wardrobe work.

LAWYER

Jackets

1. Black jacket
2. Camel gabardine jacket

Skirts

1. Camel and black tweed flare skirt
   a) black bow blouse (+ jacket 1 or 2)
   b) cream silk blouse (+ jacket 1 or 2)
2. Camel gabardine A-line skirt
   a) black bow blouse (+ jacket 2)
   b) cream silk blouse (+ jacket 1 or 2)
3. Black accordion-pleated skirt
   a) black bow blouse (+ jacket 1)
   b) cream silk blouse (+ jacket 1)
4. Camel and black checked wool straight skirt
   a) black bow blouse (+ jacket 1 or 2)
   b) cream silk blouse (+ jacket 1 or 2)

Dresses

1. Teal doubleknit dress (+ jacket 1)
2. Red wool crepe dress with black bow (+ jacket 1)

Jacket 1:   Cream silk   Jacket 2:   Black bow
Black jacket   blouse   Camel gabardine   blouse
                              jacket

*If your company is conservative
and you're an executive . . .*
you'll win their confidence
with choices like these.

Dress 1:   Teal doubleknit dress
Dress 2:   Red wool crepe dress
with black bow

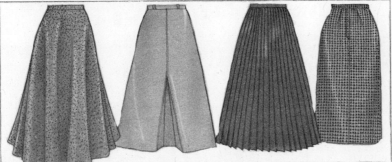

Skirt 1:   Camel and black tweed flare skirt
Skirt 2:   Camel gabardine A-line skirt
Skirt 3:   Black accordion-pleated skirt
Skirt 4:   Camel and black checked wool straight skirt

Jacket/Sweater jacket

1. Red wool blazer
2. Dark brown tweed cardigan sweater

Skirts

1. Red/yellow/purple sewn-down pleated plaid skirt
   a) pale yellow turtleneck (+ jacket 1)
   b) purple angora sweater set
   c) classic cream blouse (+ jacket 1)
2. Brown herringbone tweed skirt
   a) pale yellow turtleneck (+ jacket 1 or 2)
   b) classic cream blouse (+ jacket 1 or 2)
3. Challis print of red and purple dirndl skirt
   a) pale yellow turtleneck (+ jacket 1)
   b) purple angora sweater set
   c) classic cream blouse (+ jacket 1)
   d) matching challis print of red and purple bowed blouse (+ jacket 1)

Pants

1. Light-brown pleated pant
   a) pale yellow turtleneck (+ jacket 1 or 2)
   b) purple angora sweater set
   c) classic cream blouse (+ jacket 1 or 2)
   d) challis blouse (+ jacket 1)

Jacket 1:
Red wool blazer

Jacket 2:
Dark brown tweed
cardigan sweater

Challis print of
red and purple
bowed blouse

Classic
cream blouse

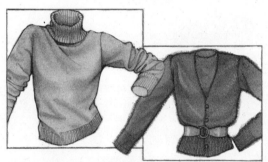

Pale yellow turtleneck

Purple angora
sweater set

*If your company is middle-of-the-road
and you're an administrative assistant . . .*
you'll find the going's great with
this kind of balance of
casual brights and more
conservative classics.

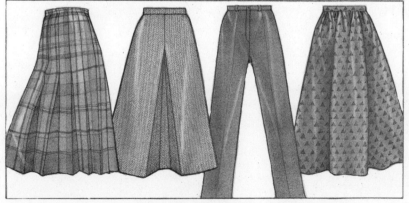

Skirt 1:   Red/yellow/purple sewn-down pleated plaid skirt
Skirt 2:   Brown herringbone tweed skirt
Pants: Light-brown pleated pants
Skirt 3:   Challis print of red and purple dirndl skirt

Shawl

1. Multicolor paisley challis shawl

Skirts
1. Burgundy tweed culotte skirt
   a) cream textured sweater (+ shawl)
   b) pale olive overblouse of rough cotton (+ shawl)
   c) dramatic white silk blouse (+ shawl)
   d) cream cotton Victorian blouse (+ shawl)
2. Cinnamon and burgundy blanket plaid flared skirt
   a) cream textured sweater
   b) pale olive rough cotton blouse
   c) white silk blouse
   d) cream cotton Victorian blouse
   e) cinnamon silk overblouse with open classic collar
3. Aztec nonseasonal heavy cotton multicolored skirt
   a) cream textured sweater
   b) pale olive rough cotton blouse
   c) white silk blouse
   d) cream cotton Victorian blouse
   e) cinnamon silk overblouse

Pants

1. Black pleated pants
   a) cream textured sweater (+ shawl)
   b) pale olive rough cotton blouse (+ shawl)
   c) white silk blouse (+ shawl)
   d) cream cotton Victorian blouse (+ shawl)
   e) cinnamon silk overblouse (+ shawl)

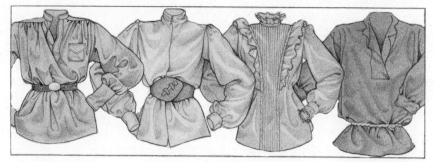

Pale olive
overblouse of
rough cotton

Dramatic
white silk
blouse

Cream cotton
Victorian blouse

Cinnamon silk
overblouse
with open collar

*If your company is way out
and you're a comer on the way up . . .
enjoy your freedom—and show it—
in stand-out clothes like these.*

Cream textured sweater
Shawl: Multicolor paisley challis shawl

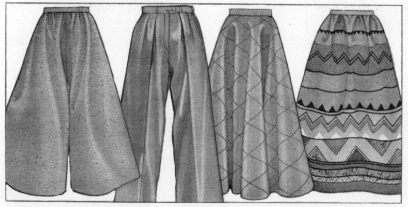

Skirt 1: Burgundy tweed culotte skirt
Pants: Black pleated pants
Skirt 2: Cinnamon and burgundy blanket plaid flared skirt
Skirt 3: Aztec nonseasonal heavy cotton multicolored skirt

*"Your outfit's
terrific—
don't blow it!"*

One of the more maddening facts of life is no matter how much thought and care you've put into your outfit, the whole effect can be ruined by one little bit of thoughtlessness, carelessness, or poor judgment. The good news is, these flaws are truly little and can be easily corrected. The important thing is to be alert. Catch them before they happen.

Don't, for instance, arrive at the office with a bra strap showing or a visible bra or panty line. Don't come in scuffed shoes, or bare legs, or stockings with a run in them. Don't wear open-toe sandals showing reinforced-toe hose. Don't wear anything with a spot on it, a hem coming down, a loose or missing button. Don't wear a coat that's supposed to be full-length but is shorter than your skirt.

Don't wear scarves in inappropriate ways. No turbans, for instance—they're too exotic. No long, trailing scarf tied around your neck—too "Isadora Duncan." And don't tie a scarf around your waist instead of a belt—it looks too makeshift and costumey.

Don't wear boots in the office. Boots are okay going to and from (be sure your skirt covers your boot-top), but not while you're at work. Keep an extra pair of all-purpose shoes at the office to change into—you'll look more professional.

Don't wear too many rings on your fingers—not more than three on both hands. The rings you do wear should be good quality classics, not distractingly ornate. Don't have your fingernails so long, people wonder out loud, "How can you *do* anything with those nails?"

Don't wear more than one bangle. You may like the look of two, but the constant jangling can be annoying to you as well as to others.

Generally speaking, you'll always be a visual asset in the office if you keep the following lists in mind:

ALWAYS RIGHT	RISKY	NEVER
Classic matched suits	Too-trendy looks	Leg o' mutton sleeves
Unmatched suits	Sloppy looks (some overblouses)	Pull-on elastic-waist pants
Blazer and coordinates	T-shirts	Jeans
Straight-leg, well-tailored pants with jacket	Faddy pants	Anything too:
	Certain culottes (too short, wide, or casual)	sheer
		tight
Shirtwaist dresses and jackets	Childish, not youthful, puffed sleeves	revealing
		low-cut
Unconstructed jackets		backless
	Midi-skirts	short
Sweater vests	Peasant blouses	Any polyester doubleknit fabric
Silk dresses (not low-cut and not ruffly)	Overmatched shoes-dress-handbag	Shiny polyester anything
	Extreme shoulder pads	Miniskirts
Well-cut knits	Extreme lapels	Evening jewelry in daytime (e.g., rhinestones)
	Extreme anything	
	Bulky or jangly jewelry	Clunky shoes
		Clunky anything

Are you working stiff because of your clothes? No matter how much you've thought about your clothes, if you can't forget about them at work, you haven't thought enough. No one can do her best work if she's not comfortable in her clothes—comfortable psychologically, comfortable physically.

Working stiff

Don't wear any item of clothing that keeps you constantly aware of it. A blouse with a too-high collar . . . a scarf that keeps coming undone . . . a neckline you have to remember not to bend over in . . . a slit skirt that falls open unless you sit just so.

One bank executive had a very expensive suit she wore to top-level meetings. The jacket closing had a snap that kept opening. It was not only a constant annoyance, but it also broke her concentration.

Test your outfit by sitting down and standing up to be sure it's completely comfortable before going to work. You might even try walking in it. One highly-placed woman in a TV network found that her slingback shoes "clonked" so loudly when she walked, everyone knew, sight unseen, who it was coming or going. Another woman had a beautiful suit blouse with a collar that followed the line of the suit to a tee. But the first time she removed the jacket and sat down, she realized the V-neck was so low she had to adjust it constantly all day. Clothes that don't work keep you tense and distracted, wasting energy you need to put into your job.

The Cinderella Switch

Going from day to evening—without going home first. Switching from business to pleasure without missing a beat. For working women these days, knowing how is a must. And savvy women everywhere have made it into a fine art. Will it be to dinner with your husband and his most important client? A new gallery opening at the museum? The annual convention of your company's sales managers at the poshest hotel in town? An out-of-the-blue invitation to the new hit play from that interesting man you met two weekends ago?

The Cinderella Switch is simpler than you think, especially if you know ahead of time where you're going. You choose an outfit that can change character with just a little sleight of hand and take along a few addables or exchangeables to complete the illusion. If you're wearing a suit, this day it'll be your pale gabardine . . . or your dressy black wool . . . or your burgundy velvet jacket with its soft wine knit skirt. Any of these is acceptable office wear, but any of them will look right in a posh restaurant, front row center at the theater, or in an after-show supper club. Wear a silk blouse with a now-you-close-it, now-you-don't collar. A neckline that works during the day with a scarf or tied bow or even just a buttoned button. After five, you'll drop the scarf or tie, unbutton the button, and wear a gold chain or interesting necklace instead.

Change your gold earrings for pearl, your workaday nylons for evening sheers, your business pumps for strippy sandals you've

The Cinderella Switch

From a good day's work   . . . to a great night's play.

brought with you. Take out the small dressy clutch you brought in your handbag.

Other possibilities? Wear a little silk camisole under your blouse—no one will see it during the day. Then wear it by itself under your suit that night. Or wear your suit jacket with nothing underneath. Or spice up a knit dress for evening with an unusual necklace or pin and earrings. Or see how a self-belted silk dress simple enough for work turns surprisingly glamorous with a switch to an important evening belt.

The thing to remember in choosing your outfit is—*it's what's up top that counts.* Because the top is what will be seen at a restaurant table or in a theater seat. (Velvet jacket, tweed skirt works; tweed jacket, velvet skirt doesn't!)

If you know you're going out, wool gabardine is a safer choice of texture than a gutsy tweed because it's not restricted to a day or night category, or a summer or winter category. A rabbit-hair blend in a knit is a better choice than a doubleknit if you might be going out after work because it is softer and can be made dressier with accessories.

A pretty, dressy belt with some glitter acts like a signal to others that you've made the effort . . . that now you're dressed up. People like signs that you care enough to do that for them.

Jewelry is the classic signal of change from day to evening—both for yourself and others—because it's the easiest to carry with you to work. Like color, it's also very easy for people to recognize and appreciate.

A well-done makeup job also sends a welcome message to others that you put some thought into this evening event. People love to see visible evidence of appropriate effort. A change of makeup probably makes you feel even better than a change of shoes or any other accessory because you simply feel prettier. That, in turn, leads to a quick lift of spirits that wipes out fatigue. Whether it's due to the glitter on your eyelids or the bareness of the camisole under your jacket, feeling glamorous will instantly turn on the energy of an attractive personality.

The key principle to remember is the more changes you make, the more they'll separate day from night. Therefore even so small a thing as a comb lifting your hair on one side over your ear will make a surprising difference. To think ahead and stick that comb in your bag in the morning will be well worth the effort, I promise.

IF YOU KNOW YOU'RE GOING OUT

1. Choose silk over cotton in the morning.
2. Choose wool gabardine over wool of any other type unless the wool is extremely soft, dressy, or black.
3. Put a dressy belt in your bag.
4. Wear slingback shoes instead of pumps, or carry your evening sandals.
5. Put a tiny evening bag in your handbag.
6. Don't forget jewelry.
7. Put nighttime makeup in your makeup case.
8. Choose a no-collar blouse.
9. Pack sheerer, dressier stockings.
10. Carry a camisole or wear a lacy one under your blouse, and undo one more button of the blouse after work.
11. Put a pretty comb in your hair.
12. Wear a shawl instead of a jacket to work; a cape instead of a coat.

INSTANT FRESHENERS AT FIVE

1. A quick spray of Evian water (adds moisture, sets makeup).
2. A gleam of bronze face powder.
3. "Instant set" done with hairspray and clips you keep in your purse.
4. A cotton ball doused with your favorite perfume to tuck inside your bra.
5. Visine for red, tired eyes.
6. Hand lotion on hands *and* feet. Adds shine and smoothness to arms and legs, gives a luxurious feel to those sheer stockings.
7. Mini deodorant.
8. Mini hairspray.

Up at bat—
dressing for the
interview

There are few times in your working life when your clothes will be as important as the outfit you wear for a new job interview. Important not only for the impact it has on the person interviewing you, but even more important for how it makes you feel about yourself. How confident you feel in it . . . how sure you are it's sending the right messages about you. It's going to be a lot easier to psych yourself up to the go-fight-win high that gets you the job if your clothes add up to a winner's look.

The first thing you have to decide is where you want to be in the spectrum from "Knock 'em dead" to "Come as you are." Jobs have been won by free spirits at either extreme—but always with a certain amount of risk. (The winning combination might well be an inspired mix of both, with a dollop of "quiet good taste" if that could be managed.)

You would dress differently if you were up for a job in an avant-garde fashion house, a Wall Street law firm, a TV production company, or a nursery school. Nevertheless there are certain general principles in deciding what to wear for an interview you should keep in mind no matter what your personality is or what kind of company you're seeing.

The first rule is your outfit should be comfortable—both physically and emotionally. I've touched on this before, but for an interview it's absolutely crucial. Nothing is worse than discovering your wrap skirt doesn't stay closed when you sit down, or your waistband is too tight, or your high-necked polyester blouse has you perspiring.

Whatever outfit you decide on, it must be tested and worn before the interview so any of these or other problems can be detected and solved. Sometimes even when you've already worn the pieces separately with no difficulty, when they are worn together, problems crop up you haven't foreseen. The sleeves of your favorite silk blouse may be soft and flowing when you wear it with just a skirt—but under a suit jacket they may bunch up uncomfortably or fall down over your knuckles.

The physical comfort of your clothes is the underpinning for the emotional comfort. And emotional comfort is largely a matter of familiarity. Wearing the tried, true, and trusted.

If you decide to create a whole new image for your interview, chances are you won't feel it's the real you, and your self-consciousness may affect the interview. If you dress "in character"—instead of "in costume"—you'll be a lot more relaxed, and your ease and poise will not only show, it'll be catching!

Maybe your interview outfit is already in your closet. If it's a look you've been wearing and are happy with, perhaps all it needs is to be freshened up with a new blouse, belt, or shoes. Or, if it's shabby, but you love it, copy it as closely as you can with new pieces. Then put them on and try them out: sit, stand, move around in them until you make them your own.

A blouse and skirt should be tied together with a jacket, sweater-jacket, or vest and accessories. That's how you get a finished look. If the skirt and blouse are of good enough quality and similar enough in color blend and fabric complement, they can be made to look as important as a dress with the addition of the proper belt and a simple necklace. And with shoes in the same color tone and the proper stockings, the look can be finished enough to stand alone, without a third layer of a jacket or vest.

A formal interview at a bank might require the safety of a suit—depending on the size and location (city or suburb) of the bank. But that doesn't have to mean a "gray flannel" suit, necessarily. It could be in a becoming color, a soft plaid or tweed (a city tweed, smooth, rather than a heavy rough country tweed). Since a suit is formal by nature, you can add color with a blouse, add softness with a bow at the neck, add fashion with a chic belt.

DO   . . . try out your outfit for comfort.

. . . have at least one other alternative to substitute in case of emergency (i.e., shoes, blouse, any part that could go wrong at the last minute).

. . . check it out the day before to make sure it's all together. Accessories too!

. . . make sure your makeup colors are appropriate for the outfit (the tone of your lipstick, blush, eyeshadow, etc.).

. . . have at least two extra pair of stockings and *carry one with you.*

. . . *get up early.* (If you're late, your clothes won't help!)

. . . put it on and forget it!!

P.S.   When you get the job, do try to keep up the same standard you were hired on.

DON'T   . . . spend your first month's salary on your interview outfit unless it can be worn over and over again for work.

. . . buy something so "un-you" that you'll never need it or wear it again.

. . . unwrap the box of new clothing and put it on the morning of the interview.

. . . wear any object or accessory that could be disconcerting—a clanking bracelet, a chain that catches, a watch with an alarm (they've been known to go off at the wrong times).

. . . wear a heel so high it will make you weave, or a heel so skinny it might catch on the carpet.

Onstage dressing   When you have to speak in front of a group on business occasions—give a presentation at a sales conference, outline a new project at a board meeting—deciding what to wear will come second only to deciding what you're going to say.

But if you're going to speak to a public group away from the office, you'll need to think about a lot of other things as well, and get as much information about the event as possible. What is the group like? The median age . . . the occupations represented . . . the socioeconomic statistics of the area. Where will the event take place? In a church? A college? A department store? A bookshop? What is the nature of your topic? What is the purpose of your talk? Is it serious or mainly for entertainment? All these considerations will have a bearing on how you dress—but the bottom line is still *be yourself.* Even if with moderation.

Special points to keep in mind:

1. *Don't* wear pants.
2. *Don't* let your appearance overpower your speech. If your clothes are too striking, your audience will be too busy looking at *them* to listen to *you.*
3. *Don't* overlook any flaw in what you wear that might undermine you on stage—a missing button, a falling hem, a missing snap, a rustling skirt, heels so high you teeter, a clanking bracelet, a necklace that dangles onto the pages of your speech, hair that falls in your eyes, a ring that rolls around on your finger, an itchy sweater, too many warm layers, an annoyingly stiff collar—in short, anything that makes you uncomfortable or distracts YOU.
4. *Do* wear a flattering, pretty color next to your face. People love to focus on color.
5. *Do* make a special effort. It will pay off.

SAMPLE CASUAL OUTFIT	SAMPLE FORMAL OUTFIT	*At ease—and in command*
Camel and burgundy tweed jacket	Burgundy matched suit	
Camel skirt	Cream silk shirt with a high ruffled neck	
Burgundy silk shirt with open collar	Narrow burgundy belt	
Luggage (caramel) belt	Sheer taupe stockings	
Skintone stockings	Burgundy pumps	
Luggage (caramel) slingback heels		

63

How far is "up"?
(dressing for the
office party)

Dressing up for the office party is one of those deceptively minor decisions that offer a chance to make a major mistake. Inappropriate behavior—often stemming from inappropriate dress—has often created such embarrassing incidents many major companies have dropped office parties entirely.

Whether or not we're aware of it, what we're wearing sometimes tends to influence our behavior. That's fine if you want to loosen up at a cocktail party with friends, but it's wise to ask yourself just how much you want to loosen up at the office party. If fellow employees see a more relaxed side of your personality, it's nothing to worry about so long as it's a *comfortable* change—both for them and for you.

If, however, you're wearing an outfit that makes you feel you have to give an explanation, like "I didn't realize this neckline was so low," or "this fabric didn't use to cling to me like this," you're probably wearing the wrong thing.

If the party is at the end of a work day, you know most people will appear in anything from the suit they wore all day to a blouse and skirt snapped up with a dressy belt and a change of jewelry. If it's a special evening event at a place away from the office, ask a fellow employee who attended last year what was worn.

The cardinal rule is to maintain the level of position you hold at the office—a softer version of your business image. Look as beautiful as you can, but never so wild or exotic or glamorous that people will from then on be a little uncertain of just who the "real" you is.

How low is
"down"?
(dressing for the
office outing)

Dressing down is tricky business. Because while you want to look casual and relaxed enough to have a good time, you still have to be sure you signal your true position in the hierarchy at work. You don't want to wear blue jeans and look like the secretary if you're not, yet you don't want to appear in a designer jumpsuit like your female boss and thereby risk offending her.

Good quality pants (make sure they fit properly and are long enough, or they could easily become office conversation) topped with a well-made blouse and an easy sweater vest, or a midi prairie skirt, belted, with a soft turtleneck and flat boots would be appropriate for an event like a company picnic.

If most of the women will be wearing basic pants, make sure your top has character and interest. Don't lose this opportunity to show a different side of your character, perhaps ethnic or more kooky. Leave it to the quality to signify your position in the hierarchy.

Dressing for business travel is the science—and art—of taking the least amount of clothes that will cover the widest variety of occasions. (And not forgetting anything you need.)

It goes without saying that the less you carry the easier travel will be. Yet you'll want to be dressed right for anything—from morning conferences to cocktail-dinner receptions. How well you bring this off depends on two things: keeping it simple and coordinating your colors.

The secret is to start at the bottom—coordinate your clothing around no more than two pairs of shoes. An ideal travel wardrobe, increased or decreased according to length of stay, would look like this:

1. A dark suit (dark so it could be dressed up or down).
2. An alternate skirt for the suit jacket.
3. Two blouses—one dressy, one casual.
4. A silk dress that could be worn under the suit jacket or on its own.
5. A medium-weight gabardine coat in a neutral color to fit over the suit jacket.
6. Two handbags—the one you carry by day and a smaller one for evening.
7. Two pairs of shoes—pumps and an alternate, e.g., slingbacks in a different color.
8. Four pairs of stockings—one sheer for evening.
9. Dressy accessories for after five: pearls, dressy belt for suit skirt and/or dress, other jewelry for day changes (nothing, alas, you can't afford to have stolen).

The selection above will work well for almost any business trip of three or four days.

Just to illustrate the thought process, here's how a suit, a skirt, a dress, and a couple of blouses can mix and match into eight complete outfits.

SUIT Burgundy A-line skirt with its burgundy short jacket
    a. daytime look: burgundy and gray stripe cotton shirt
    b. dressy look: gray silk blouse with ruffled neckline
    c. day to evening look: top of dress listed below (burgundy-gray paisley cossack top)

SKIRT Unmatched burgundy-gray tweed with burgundy suit jacket (above)
    a. same burgundy and gray stripe cotton shirt
    b. same gray silk blouse with ruffled neckline
    c. top of dress (same burgundy-gray paisley cossack top)

DRESS Burgundy-gray paisley two-piece silk with cossack top, sewn-down pleated skirt, with or without burgundy suit jacket (above) over dress

When you're back from your first trip, make a list of things you forgot to take. Add them to the original list of things you packed and just pull out the list each time you need to take a trip. Better yet, tape it to the inside of your suitcase.

In any case, whatever you forget, there's seldom need for panic. Unless you've been sent to Timbuctoo on an hour's notice, you can probably get whatever you need, wherever you are. Case in point: One friend had to leave unexpectedly from her office on a business trip that would keep her in conference rooms every day from nine to five for three days. She had nothing with her and no time to go home. How did she handle it? On her first lunch break, she found out the name of the largest department store in town. As she'd hoped, they had a personal shopper. This savvy lady came up with a blouse and extra skirt to coordinate with the jacket she traveled in, along with underwear, stockings, toilet articles, and nightgown. The whole package was charged to her account (a check with identification would have been accepted) and delivered by messenger to her hotel.

The no-panic good sense with which my friend handled this surprise crisis is the same good sense she shows in her job and why her company prizes her so highly.

- Brush and comb, shower cap, curlers, toothbrush and toothpaste, shaving equipment, bath powder
- Underwear, several pairs of stockings, nightgown, slippers, robe
- Makeup, cotton balls, perfume
- Glasses, contact lenses (extra pair)
- Credit cards, travelers checks, single dollars, loose change, phone numbers
- "Loseable" jewelry
- Book
- Small notebook and pen to carry in your purse to record expenses, people's names, interesting places you've been

DRESSING YOUR WAY OUT OF CONFLICT PROBLEMS

How to dress younger . . . without looking as if you were trying too hard may well be the neatest trick of all in an era when more women over thirty-five are going back to work than ever before . . . when youth seems to be an absolute must in forging ahead in business . . . and when society aims its cruelest jeers at women who try too desperately to look young. But you *can* do it.

Dressing younger without trying too hard

Pretty colors are the fastest way to signal joy and fun—characteristics of the young. If you have a closetful of dull safe solids, give your wardrobe a healthy infusion of lively colors and prints. And shed a few years.

Unmatched suits look young. (A coordinated, but finished look in separates is even younger. A smashing short sweater, for instance, that ties together a full longer skirt and wool challis ruffled blouse.) A mix of textures look young. Each in its own way expresses the outlook of the young—the daring to experiment, the love of individuality, the delight in the unexpected.

Short jackets, bloused or fitted to the waist, or peplum jackets, tight at the waist, flared over the hips, give a younger look because they project the cute pert image compared to large out-of-proportion jackets.

67

Softer fabrics, more inviting to the touch, are younger than hard, tailored fabrics. Men's dry tweeds or strict pinstripes give the oldest image.

Shoes with slingback heels that show more foot are sexier and therefore younger than closed pumps. Lighter-weight higher pumps are younger than heavy-looking low pumps.

In sum, when it comes to looking younger, these are the things to remember:

Softer fabrics	Soft collars worn open
A mix of textures	Crushy belts
Pretty shades of colors	Slingback shoes
Unmatched suits	Coordinated—but not perfectly
Un-stiff jackets	matched—shoes and bag
Short blouson or peplum tops	
And	
No wardrobe of dull, mousy	Less hair spray
colors	Softer makeup
No gaudy jewelry	Nonglaring nail polish
No outfit totally devoid of	
accessories	

Dressing more authoritatively without looking old

How to dress more authoritatively . . . without looking old is the *second* neatest trick of all—especially for women who spent their youth being, and looking, soft and sweet. To gain more authority, the most important principle to remember is to wear finer quality, more sophisticated subtle lines and coloring.

The better the quality, the more subtle the coordinating seems to get. In a coordinated costly silk two-piece print dress, there is sometimes such a subtle difference in prints you can hardly tell they are different. Yet something about the combination is more interesting than if it were the same print. In separates of all different textures, the more sophisticated the woman, the more the outfit has a oneness of color. Or, if not in one color, than in one mood, i.e., dusty rusts and dusty greens, or pale pink with pale beige worn with cream pearls.

For more authority, keep in mind:

- Wear quality.
- Wear a jacket to work—the higher the quality, the more authority.
- Wear subtle, sophisticated colors, or if you look smashing in a bright color like electric blue, wear it occasionally.
- Wear small sophisticated prints, geometrics, rather than large flowers.
- Carry a fine leather handbag—your most important accessory— not trendy, but classic.
- Always have finishing touches to your outfit—a belt to look pulled-together even when you take off your jacket, a small pair of earrings, perhaps a gold chain at your neck.
- Wear good quality jewelry if you afford it, and if you can't, a fine costume copy.
- Always keep the same high standard to your look.

Can you wear pink and still be boss?

There's pink . . . and there's pink. And *quality* makes the difference. If you choose your fabrics carefully, chances are the manufacturers of quality goods will already have thought out the problem for you. To begin with, quality goods take dyes better. Chances are also that those same manufacturers have chosen muted versions of your favorite pink—and muted versions of most other "problem" colors like baby blue, violet, etc. Muted or "off" shades lend quality to the look of a garment. A mauvey pink is subtle. So is dusty pink. And muted fuchsia. ("Powder pink" and "shocking pink" are the ones to stay away from.) "Facepowder pink"—a muted alabaster shade of pink—is fine, and so is a small geometric print with a touch of shocking pink. And if you're going to wear shocking pink, keep it in a small quantity.

Pink in itself will not diminish your stature if it is in as good taste as the rest of your wardrobe. Becoming boss doesn't mean saying goodbye to femininity—or to pink. Or to any other fashion you may happen to love. If you're comfortable in it, wear it. *But with style.*

69

*Breaking the mold
vs. dressing true
to type*

Is it ever wise to shake people up? Yes, depending on when you do it, where you do it, *how* you do it. If people think of you in stereotype—"She's such a nice girl" . . . "No-nonsense Nan" . . . "*Cosmo* sexpot" . . . "Old Faithful"—it's good for you, and good for them, to put a few holes in their preconceived notions. But keep in mind what you're aiming for: happy surprise, not seismic shock. Stereotypes are *comfortable.* That's why it's so easy for people to slide into them, and change can often be uncomfortable. So when you shake them up, try to keep the discomfort quotient down and the intriguing difference up.

If they've thought of you for five years as the girl next door, showing up as a *Cosmo* Sexpot one morning may startle everybody all right—for the first hour, say—but in the long run, they just won't believe your transformation. Make your changes more subtle. They'll still be noticed and, over time, they'll have more impact.

When the occasion permits—a special client meeting, an office function, lunch with the staff, a business trip—try something a little more daring and stylish. Even the addition of color, if your working wardrobe is mostly browns and beiges, can do the trick and give you instant relief from feeling like a fly in amber, caught inside a static self-image . . . the only self the office ever sees. And that slight variation may give upper management a clue that you're more creative than they thought.

Perhaps the most important standard to strive for in dressing for the job is "appropriateness." Distinction, drama, style, individuality, good taste are all important and desirable. But none of them will take the place of appropriateness.

In the world of style, appropriateness is not exactly an exciting word, but for a working woman, nothing is more vital. Because nothing shows her good sense and judgment more clearly . . . nothing confirms that she's in control more surely . . . nothing weighs so heavily in how others size up her ability on the job.

Ironically enough, in most jobs, appropriateness can mean "don't look too perfect." If you do, you can communicate the message that you really care more about turning yourself out than doing your job well. The only exception is if your job is in the fashion field. In that case, looking perfect means you really know your work.

Dress well for every company function—from board meeting to annual picnic—because you're on display. Use the arena; it's not only a challenge, it's an opportunity. Always remember it's more important to represent the company and its product in the way you dress than to express your daily moods, whether you want to hide from the world one day in a mousy suit or flaunt your femininity in a see-through blouse the next. If you're in sales, never lose sight of the fact that in a very fundamental sense you *are* your product. Your customer's opinion of your product will be heavily influenced by his opinion of you. If you look good, the product looks better to him. If you don't look good, the product has less of a chance.

FROM "UNDER ORDERS" TO "IN CHARGE"

When you're promoted from underling to boss, you'll be going through one of the most delicate and difficult transitions you'll face in the working world. The change in role requires so many other changes, inside and out—not only in you, but in the people around you. Especially if the change is abrupt—when only yesterday you were one of the Indians, running the errands, and today you're the Chief, running the show.

Of course you'll need to make a change in the way you dress, but the most important thing is to *make the change slowly.* Let the people you work with become aware gradually that you're dressing differently, looking better, projecting a more authoritative fashion image. Don't knock them out with a fashion statement so loud and strong, they'll think you're throwing your weight around, showing off your new role. They won't be comfortable with the new you. And more important, neither will you. Clothing can enhance success— but it doesn't determine it.

Mary E. worked for several years in a linen shop with two women. When they decided to sell, Mary—much to everybody's surprise, including her own—made a bid and became the owner of the store. The previous owners stayed on part-time as her employees along with the rest of the staff.

Mary, who had dressed mainly in skirts or pants and sweaters and shirts, knew she needed to make a big change. She needed "instant authority." She now had to meet the public as an owner and deal with the manufacturers' representatives. Her first change was from cardigan sweaters to easy jackets. The jackets created authority and pulled together her skirts, pants, and tops. Another change was an upgrade in fabrics. Instead of polyester blouses, she began to invest in silk. She also added several good leather belts and shoes. Since the transition was literally "overnight," she didn't want to feel as if she were dressed up in her mother's clothes. By adding to her own, and accessorizing, she was comfortable and the transition was smooth.

As her employees came to accept her as the boss, it became easier to get a little more daring. She began to try interesting new color and fabric combinations that were less conventional, but more to her liking. She enjoyed that particular privilege of being boss.

Dressing for your public when you're in business for yourself

What kind of business you are in has a great deal to do with how you ought to dress, because the image of the business is largely colored by the image *you* project.

Jane W. went into business with Kay L. to sell photography as decorative art for the home. Her questions covered all the relevant points: "Should I look rich?" "Should I look intellectual?" "Should I look arty?" Since the fundamental product of their business was good taste—that was really what their customers paid for—she decided this was the quality her clothes should reflect at all times. Also to be considered was the fact that her clients varied from large corporations to individuals.

Jane decided on three basic looks—that ever-reliable rule for a wardrobe that works. A formal matched suit for major presentations. A coordinated skirt for the jacket for less formal presentations. An "easy" dress that could be worn with the jacket as needed, another option.

The wardrobe was based on a combination of needs. Obviously the business had to be represented with authority, hence the suit. Yet she had to be approachable to her individual clients, hence the softened look.

As in every job, once you've established yourself and the value of your company, you are free to move into looks that are more expressive of your own personal style—the style that develops through your own self-confidence and the recognition that comes your way.

Don't let your clothing block your success. Don't let your clothing slow it up by projecting a person that is not *you*—a person you'll have to disown later on. It's too much of a battle while you're proving your competence on the job.

HOW TO GET DRESSED IN THE MORNING

Even if you think you mastered getting dressed when you were six, there may still be room for improvement. How you handle morning rush hour—whether it's only you, or all five of you—can set the tone for the whole day. If you're behind schedule before you even go out the door, chances are you'll spend the whole day trying to catch up, apologizing as you go. If however, you leave in good time with everything under control, your self-confidence and security will be intact for everything you do. You'll look better to yourself—and to the world.

The trick to getting dressed in the morning is absurdly simple. *Start the night before.* Take the decisions out of the process. Put out all items you're going to wear, including accessories—jewelry, belts, shoes. Check to be sure no repairs are necessary. (If it's raining and your boots are black, it may affect which outfit you want to wear that day, even if you'll be removing your boots at the office.) Check contents of purse to be sure everything you'll want in the morning is there, including special phone numbers for calls you're going to make, sales slips for things you might be returning after work, etc. Lay out anything you have to take to the office: reading matter, reports, a special relevant article you've clipped.

In the morning:

1.	Go out for your morning run	20 minutes to dress and run
2.	Shower, comb hair	10 minutes
3.	Put on robe, have breakfast	10 minutes
4.	Put on makeup	10 minutes
5.	Get half-dressed—underwear, stockings, shoes, skirt	10 minutes
6.	Make bed, do any organizing necessary	5 minutes
7.	Put on blouse, jacket, accessories	5 minutes

(Don't forget to check yourself in a full-length mirror.)

This is only one possible scenario, best probably for a live-alone with easy-to-manage hair that calls for only a combing. If you have problem hair that needs to be set or blow-dried every morning, you'll need a longer schedule. Ditto if you have children to feed or get off to school. Or a husband who can never find his socks.

The important thing is not what your schedule consists of or how long it takes, but that you've got it down so you can do it in your sleep. (Some days you probably *will* do it in your sleep.) If there's one thing you owe yourself in the morning—especially if you're not a "morning person"—it's the luxury of not having to think about what you're doing. Do it in the same order each time and you won't have to. The more you perfect your routine, the longer you can let your mind snooze on hold.

SAVE THE DAY WARDROBE KIT FOR OFFICE EMERGENCIES

1. Needles and thread of several colors, safety pins in two sizes
2. Extra pantyhose in several shades
3. Colorless nail polish to stop runs
4. Nail clipper and file
5. Chalk-type spot remover
6. Comb
7. Clothes brush
8. Good-looking tote for lunch hour purchases
9. Fold-up raincoat for unforeseen cloudbursts
10. Extra pair of all-purpose shoes

5

YOUR SUPPORT SYSTEM

(Your Wardrobe, Your Shopping, Your Closets):

How to Set It Up So It Won't Let You Down

A good wardrobe should cover your life—as well as your body—comfort your purse . . . bail you out of emergencies . . . bring out your best self . . . give a lift to your soul . . . and beam out messages of shameless approval about you like a doting mother.

And it will—but you've got to set it up that way with the three-part support system that will keep you dressed right 365 days a year. Planning your wardrobe. Shopping well. Setting up your closets.

WARDROBE PLANNING—THE GRAND STRATEGY

The overriding thing about a working woman's wardrobe is it has to *work*. Nonstop. It has to stay in fashion on a continuing basis. It has to take the minimum amount of time and effort—both in getting it together and in upkeep. It has to be varied and versatile, covering all the lives you lead. And making you feel good in all of them.

The first step is to take a look at your life and see how—and where—you spend your time. Is it simply office, home, home, office? Or is it work, home, parties, parent-teacher conferences, weekends, business trips, vacation trips? Is it sales meetings, seminars, public speaking, theater going, restaurant dining, cocktail parties, and balls? Is it a low-key mixture of a few of the above or a high octane mix of just about all of them?

Make a list of your activities—you may surprise yourself. Compare it with last year's and make another list. How many times last year did your wardrobe fail you? When and where did you wish you were wearing something more daring—or less self-conscious? When and where did you feel you weren't doing justice to the occasion—or to yourself? When and where did you arrive wearing your safe, all-purpose party dress when everyone else was dressed all-out?

Then make a list of the recurring events in your life, in their order of importance for your being well-dressed. One of the commonest traps you can fall into as a working woman is to spend all your energy and money on getting clothes for the office and finding you have nothing but jeans and T-shirts for the rest of your life. And only one dress for weddings, bar mitzvahs, graduations, and other such high points.

Consider too your husband's preferences, position, lifestyle. Is he a rising young lawyer slated for partnership, or is he a TV producer who spends his life in jeans on location? Is he president of his own company who likes to entertain often and regally, or a shy poet who feels you are all the people he needs for rest and recreation? Who he is and what he does will have a bearing on the clothes you choose.

In times past, dressing was easier. The '40s, the '50s, even the '60s all had their "uniforms"—the black dress and pearls, the stiff lined linen shifts, the petticoats and nipped waistlines—which made for a certain peace of mind, but at the cost of a certain constriction of spirit. In the periods of transition between "uniforms" we teetered on the brink of total confusion.

Today, there's no reason to worry. Between uniform and anarchy, there's a huge middle ground of *your* look. Ground that feels safe under your feet. And gives you lots of room to experiment. Here's how to make the most of it.

Wardrobes that work for different women may be as varied as the women themselves. But analyze what makes them work, and chances are you'll find it's the same five basics: (1) separates, (2) year-round fabrics, (3) year-round colors, (4) balance and proportion, (5) adding at least one new silhouette a year.

One and one makes three

In the wonderful world of separates, the whole is greater than the sum of its parts. And keeps on getting greater—to make you look great all the time. The way we live now calls for an easier, more flexible way of dressing. Separates fill the bill on all counts. They give you the widest freedom to evolve your own style. In subtle ways they make you look younger, more contemporary, more *individual* than a "prepackaged" outfit. They're a time-and-money-saving way to keep your wardrobe constantly refreshed, renewed. And they make you look as if you have lots more clothes than you do.

One young client coming to us fresh out of college—"almost naked," having lived for four years in T-shirts and jeans—was stunned to discover how far a few skirts, blouses, jackets could take her. The separates we chose—two jackets, four skirts, five blouses, three sweaters, two vests, two pants—mixed and matched into 114 outfits! It would be almost four months before she had to wear any outfit a second time.

Of course, dressing in separates takes more thought, but it gives you more fashion mileage for your dollar. And helps you build your wardrobe from one season to the next.

Note: If you feel you must have at least one "suit" suit for exceptionally formal business occasions, get the most expensive, high-quality suit you can afford. It should project an image of power no ordinary suit can pretend to (if it doesn't, you haven't got your money's worth). Some women armor themselves in ordinary suits because they feel "safe"—how could you be wrong wearing a suit to a business office? But ordinary suits fail you two ways. They carry no clout, and they're not even much fun.

Nonstop fabrics for on-the-go living

More of your clothes will be out in the world on you instead of hanging in the closet by themselves if you make a point of choosing transitional fabrics: wool jersey, challis, lightweight wool, flannel and gabardine; rayon, crepe, silk. These are wearable three-fourths of the year. And if they make up at least three-fourths of your separates, you'll have a wardrobe with very few pieces out of action

78

during the year—except for the hottest days of summer or the coldest days of winter.

Year-round colors—your third ace in the hole—also keep your clothes on duty at all times. Red, navy, periwinkle blue, purple, olive, cocoa, camel, beige, medium and light gray, black, and cream are appropriate in any season.

Colors that work year-round

(But it isn't only fabric that makes a piece wearable at any time of year. The fabric may be the right weight, but the color of the print, say, may be too hot-looking for summer. Or the color may be right, but the cut of the dress is too covered-up and hot-looking, so just be sensible about it.)

Ever notice how the best hairdressers make you stand up before they start cutting your hair? They want to see the proportion of your head to your body. Designers also concentrate on proportion, try to make top and bottom balance. If the top is bigger, the fabric is likely to be lighter. An eye for proportion and balance should run through your entire wardrobe—not only in line and color, but in psychology. Balance an inexpensive outfit with one expensive focal point—an inexpensive skirt and vest with a pretty print blouse of good quality, for instance. (Just make sure the focal point is in the same mood.) Balance ambition with good taste. Don't wear one designer's entire line on your back—it will seem arrogant. Or cowardly. Balance your lack of stature with formality. Balance soft muscle tone and a lack of presence with more quality and clothes that are tailored. Balance an athletic body, an aggressive manner, with less structured clothes, pretty colors, more flow in the silhouette.

Proportion and balance— the most basic basics

Each season look for one new silhouette you can meld into your existing wardrobe. It's the easiest way to keep yourself looking up-to-date. A spare pull-on natural yarn sweater (instead of the oversized bulkies you've been wearing). Or a prairie skirt with a kicky flounce to update your skirt wardrobe of strict gabardine A-lines. The one thing to avoid is the avant-garde silhouette that calls for a whole new set of accessories—even a new hairstyle to carry it off.

Automatic update

Jacket and Pants

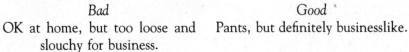

| *Bad* | *Good* |
| OK at home, but too loose and slouchy for business. | Pants, but definitely businesslike. |

One last word. Decide before you start how much comfort means to you. Some smashing clothes just aren't comfortable—even if that means they're just so expensive you're not comfortable! If you find yourself going through arguments in your head each time you're considering wearing a particular outfit, it will probably spend more

Vest and Skirt

Bad
Too "off-duty" for the job.

Good
Trim and together for work.

time in the closet than on you. As a working woman, you can't afford to waste one watt of energy being annoyed by a collar that binds, wool that scratches, skirts you can't walk in, clothes that make you too hot, clothes that don't keep you warm enough, shoes that make your feet hurt.

Jacket and Skirt

Bad
Too much "puffery" in skirt,
sleeve, and bow.

Good
Understated and everything in scale.

Jacket over Dress

Bad
Too limp. No zip or energy.

Good
Professional and polished. Young
and lively.

Start at the heart. On a limited budget—and who, these days, has anything but?—the heart of your wardrobe will be the jacket, especially if you're working. It will be the most important and expensive thing you buy, so make it the highest quality you can afford. (It should also be the most basic, which means the most versatile and therefore most wearable.) Whether it's part of a suit, or a jacket on its own, be sure it can go over several different skirts. Variety in colors and patterns should be introduced in the less expensive pieces in your wardrobe.

Don't feel yourself limited to the usual tailored blazer. There are so many other jacket shapes to choose from. The cardigan, for instance, with a jewel neckline. It falls straight, without buttons, and can be short or long. There's the easier shirt jacket, or a blouson jacket. Just avoid the gigantically overscaled ones. (If you wear fuller skirts, you'll find the shorter jacket that stops at your waist or hipbones looks better.)

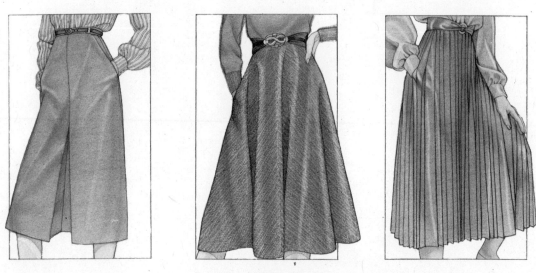

Three Good Skirts

Inverted Pleat . . . Bias . . . Accordion Pleated
Count on them for variety, a nice change of pace. All give you ease
of movement, figure flattery, long fashion-life.

Jackets that don't work

Beware of "one-shot" jackets like these. They don't mix and match. You can't leave them open. You can't build a wardrobe on them.

Jackets that do

These jackets work almost all the time, almost any place. Look good open or closed—and with all kinds of separates.

Gentle jersey   Tailored gabardine

A good rule to make life easy is to buy a solid jacket—a black velvet, say—to go with most of your tweed or patterned skirts and pants. And buy another jacket, of a different shape, in a pattern, i.e., a subtle tweed or plaid, to go with the other half of your wardrobe, the skirts and pants that are solid. That way if you stay within two color families that are compatible and can intermix, you will always be able to finish each outfit with a jacket. It's like a family tree that branches out from two important bloodlines.

Subtly striped silk

Next a pretty blouse and skirt that match. Together, they can look as important as a dress, but as separates they'll be wearable in so many different ways. Get them in any subtle interesting color you won't get tired of: plum, cinnamon, greige, pale moss. Get a soft sweater and pants in a complementary color (cinnamon/pale yellow or taupe/rose) and you'll have four pieces to mix and match in endless variety. A tweed jacket that goes with all four items will take you even further.

You'll want at least two dresses you feel good in—one that takes you from work to dinner with equal chic, the second to replace yesteryear's "basic black." Today it can be a pretty silk—discreetly ruffled blouse with a flippy skirt—in a color you love, a color that makes you feel feminine and special. If it's going to be the only dressy dress you have, don't choose a loud color or bold print, people will remember it too easily. And wonder when you're going to get another one.

The next essential is a good simple cloth coat that works well on the job and off. The trick is to find one that's slim, so you don't feel bulky and clumsy in it, but with enough room in the shoulders to go over your jackets. Choose a color that goes with as much of your wardrobe as possible. But sometimes it's worth sacrificing a little versatility for a color that gives you a lift—a cherry burgundy or a forest green, for instance.

Not many women these days can afford different color shoes for each outfit, as they did in the '40s, so get shoes and bags in two basic, yet different, color families—taupe or luggage (caramel), or burgundy or black—that go with as many outfits as possible.

In choosing a bag, the first thing to consider is its proportion to your body. Too many small women let themselves be saddled with oversized bags that overwhelm them. If you must carry a briefcase, get a small clutch that fits into it. Or get a shoulder bag. Make sure the strap is neither too long or too short. The bag should hit somewhere by your hipbone. Don't carry woven straw bags or canvas totes to work. They don't look professional.

The arts and crafts of color

I've read many color specialists' theories on which colors a person should wear, but I still don't believe in looking at the inside of your lip for your best shade of red, as one color authority once advised a client of mine. Whether a color looks good on you or not depends so much on the amount you have on and the density of the fabric.

Many clients have told me they hate olive green. But when they try on the latest cotton safari jumpsuit—which happens to look authentic only in khaki olive—they change their minds. In red or turquoise, perhaps their most flattering colors in another look, like a

88

pretty silk dress, it doesn't work nearly as well. The character of the garment changes the color it looks best in—and which looks best on *you*. Most people, I believe, can wear ninety percent of all colors. It's the shade and intensity that make a color flattering or not.

Different combinations of colors bring about a totally different effect. For instance, burgundy and rust together, or electric blue and bright red, or jade green and off-white. Different responses are evoked too. It may be a question of balance again.

If you dislike one of the colors, but like the interesting effect of the two together, wear more of the favored color and wear it next to your face. When clients tell me they won't ever wear a certain color, I take it under advisement—but I don't write it off. A bit of that color may be very interesting in a print. The client usually "doesn't count" that when I point it out to her. So don't have a closed mind on this subject.

The old rule was not to choose colors too similar to your own complexion and hair color. An ash blonde did not wear taupes, a redhead never appeared in pink or dark red. Yet a client of ours whose complexion and hair color is all ruddy and warm rust looks smashing in her rust rabbit-hair turtleneck dress and red fox fur coat flung over her shoulders. The match stunningly brings out her unique coloring and has become a most effective signature.

Color can change your complexion. Some faces come alive surrounded by clear bright colors. Others, interestingly enough (usually softer personalities), become washed out and need the help of quieter color. Constantly check your wardrobe for a balance of interesting prints and new colors. It's the easiest way to show creativity. You don't have to experiment with a new silhouette, just the same style in a brand new color of the season. Each season the fashion industry pushes a group of new colors and there is a correspondingly larger selection of fashions in those particular shades to draw from. The wide availability makes the new colors more comfortably familiar—yet they're new enough to the eye to be exciting.

If you find you can't use all the clothes in your closet it's most probably because the colors don't go together. An easy rule you can count on is that light and dark shades of the identical color go well together, i.e., a dark teal suit with a pale teal blouse. But be sure you're on the same spectrum of teal. If you go off, it may be too green a teal or too blue a teal. You might think all blacks would match, or all whites. But sometimes they are the hardest of all because there are so many shades of each. Then too, different fabrics pick up the same dye shade differently, another reason to match your colors carefully in daylight.

On the matter of balance—to my eye the balance is more pleasing when the darker color is worn on the bottom. The balance becomes perfect when a woman in a cream skirt and black blouse slips into her light cream jacket. Until then, she would look top-heavy to me, unless she had some light touch of a flower or scarf on top.

According to John T. Molloy, author of *Dress for Success*, a businesswoman wearing a light two-piece suit should wear a high-contrast dark blouse or scarf at the neck to project power. I don't agree. Sometimes if the contrast is not so strong, if the blouse is just a shade lighter than the suit, or the print of the blouse is the same color as the suit (i.e., a gray flannel suit with a lighter gray silk blouse, or a beige suit with a blouse in a small print of beige and camel), the whole outfit comes off in better taste. And the person who shows the better taste will be projecting the most power.

Color can do so much in so many ways. Use color to get you out of moods or to evoke moods in others. At dreary times in your life, cheer yourself up with color. Color is the quickest way to get a compliment from a man. Men react immediately to lively colors, especially if they see you in neutrals every day. Colors help set clear parameters. You can't be brash, boisterous in soft dusty pink.

Warm bright colors give activity to an outfit because they seem to move forward. Some colors make one come alive. On the job, sprinkle the more practical colors of your office wardrobe with occasional bright colors in a blouse or silk dress. Touches of contrasting color can be considered an accessory, like a third layer; a finishing note to an ensemble, a wine velvet collar on a brown coat-dress, for instance. If a garment's color is solid rather than a pattern, good tailoring is more important because it's more visible. If the color or print is bright and outstanding, the line of the outfit should be simpler. Cotton blouses can be worn all year round if the color is not too dark and hot for summer, or light and airy for winter. A smoky shade of eyeshadow matching the color you're wearing makes you look really pulled together.

Accessories can often make or break your look. They can be subtle or striking. They can differentiate the classes (costume jewelry vs. real gold or diamonds). They can hold a garment together physically (a pin on a wrap kilt or a plunging neckline). They can tie a whole outfit together visually. A rose-colored silk bowed-tie worn on a cream shirt can pick up a hint of pink in a tweed suit. Navy earrings to pick up on a navy in a print may just tie your whole look together. Or accessories can subtly "finish" a look—the touch of a classic gold earring and gold chain on a dark foulard print dress. They can easily update last year's look—when you add a this-season important belt. (There is no less expensive way to feel up-to-date.) They can telegraph your uniqueness. Case in point, artist Louise Nevelson, who for years has worn only black as a background for exotic jewelry.

Accessories— instant finish, pick-up, change-over, drama

To be most effective, all the accessories you wear at one time should tie together in one mood. A gutsy leather belt, a handcrafted turquoise necklace, and leather boots. Or a beautiful, delicate lace collar, the touch of a real gardenia, pearl earrings, ballet-type low-heel pumps.

The color of an accessory can either coordinate an outfit or add a necessary punch of contrast. If you are all in gray—a gray knit dress, gray-tint hose, and gray pumps—it might be exciting to wear a bright red cummerbund belt and an additional echo of red in your stickpin at your collar. It's a good rule of thumb that any color in an accessory should be supported and balanced by one more touch of that same color in another accessory. Any more than two touches may be too much; a red handbag, red shoes, and red belt would look too contrived.

Keep your accessories in scale to the silhouette of your outfit. If you're wearing a voluminous cape, it can stand a heavy ornament. A lean peplum jacket would demand something lighter. If you yourself are small, a lot of big accessories are not for you. For your proportions one accessory may be enough. If you are large, tiny delicate jewelry isn't going to do anything for you—even in quantity. If anything, it may look puzzlingly incongruous. Accessories should play up your good points, play down your bad points, to put all of you in the best possible light.

For instance: If you've got a waist to be proud of—long *and* small—sash it always with wide interesting belts. Make them your signature.

If your blue-green eyes are your best feature, jade earrings will make them even more striking. So will dusty olive eye shadow. You could plan the colors of your whole wardrobe around the color of your eyes. However, if you have blue eyes, don't wear light blue. Teal blues will play them up in a more sophisticated way.

If you've always been told you have pretty legs, wear flattering heels—not too low or too high for the office—beautifully shaped pumps, or slingbacks that show off a little more foot. Good looking shoes attract eyes to the leg.

If your hands aren't as young and pretty as you would wish, don't call attention to them with too many rings or bracelets. If you don't want to attract eyes to your bosom, don't cluster a lot of pins in the vicinity.

ACCESSORIES

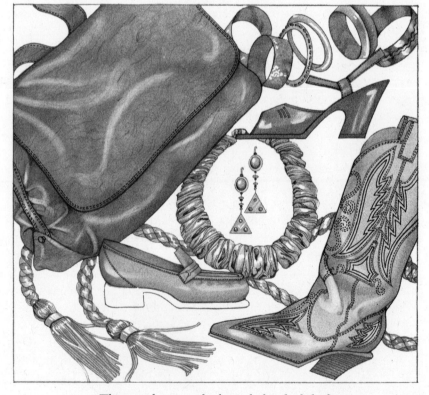

These make even the best clothes look bad
. . . extreme shapes, gross detailing, shoddy materials.

These make even modest clothes look better
. . . clean lines, fine detailing and quality materials.

If your waist is too big, don't feel you have to give up that finishing touch to your outfit. You can still wear a belt with a good-looking buckle as a focal point if you cover your sides with an open jacket or vest. If your neck is large, don't ring it with a choker as if to measure it. Wear chains that bring the focus down. Or wear only earrings instead.

If your face isn't your best feature, don't put all your money in eye-catching earrings. Place the focus on belts, a long necklace, or bracelets. Just as your hairstyle should not repeat your face shape, neither should your hat or your collar or neckline. If you have a long face, you shouldn't wear high-crowned hats, V-necks, or long hanging straight hair.

If you're large, don't signal your entrance with clanging bracelets or heavy-heeled shoes.

Quality—how to show it, how to tell it

When you're checking out a garment for quality, here are some of the things to look for:

Seams—Are they puckered? Is the stitching even? Is the thread the right color?

Collars—Are they cut to lie flat? Are both sides cut the same? (If the collar won't stay down and the clerk says it "just needs pressing," have it pressed before you take it home!)

Pockets—Are they sewn in properly? Do they show through in front? Do they bulk?

Buttonholes—Are they big or small enough for the buttons? Are they all even? Is the stitching and finishing raggedy?

Zippers—Are they set in properly? Do they pucker? Do they *zip*? Do they meet the waistband?

Prints—Do they match at the seam? Is the pattern imperfect somewhere? Is that distracting?

Colors—Do skirt and jacket match exactly? If not, it's a dye-lot difference. They were dyed at different times.

Slubs—These are imperfections in the fabric. Are they too noticeable?

Linings—Are they poorly constructed or badly fitted?

Shoulder pads—Are they poorly placed? Or too large? Too lumpy?

Seam allowance—Is there enough extra fabric in the seams for alterations? Or to allow for stress from wearing?

The hang of the skirt—Is the hem uneven?

Care instructions—Are they attached?

Fabrics—Do they have a good "hand," that is, a good feel? Do they wrinkle when you crush them even briefly?

Fabrics that say quality at its very best are the natural ones: one hundred percent cotton, silk, wool, and linen. You can't go wrong with any of these. Some of the blends—cotton and polyester, silk and polyester, wool and polyester—will also measure up if the natural fiber is by far the largest percentage of the mix.

BODY TYPES—HOW TO MAKE THE MOST OF YOURS

IF YOU ARE SHORT:

- Keep your weight down—weight just compounds your height problem.
- Shop ahead—in March and August—when stocks of clothes are at their widest.
- Wear simple lines, small prints—you don't have enough display area for large ones.
- Keep accessories simple, never too large or gaudy.
- Shop junior departments and boys' departments for sports separates, pants, shirts, etc. (Over thirty, intersperse your wardrobe with a few better-quality "grown-up" clothes.)
- European clothes are usually cut in smaller proportions—prices higher, but quality better.
- Not too long a hem length, and not too heavy a shoe, because both will bring the focus downward.
- Keep color in one family, including shoes and stockings—strong contrasts break up height.
- You can wear current and avant-garde clothes like someone tall, if you're slim and in good proportion. But the clothes must be cut to *your* right proportions. Even midi-skirts are fine, if not too long.

IF YOU ARE TALL:

- Designer clothes are usually cut with longer proportions.
- Flared skirts add grace to your height, straight skirts exaggerate it.
- And you're long-waisted, wear wide, exciting belts.
- And your legs are long, wearing big tops or blousing them balances proportion.
- Turn-back cuffs are a good casual solution to long sleeves that are too short.
- Avoid two-piece dresses with short tops—skin or slip will show when you move.
- Tiny prints, feminine ruffles, or too delicate jewelry will exaggerate your height.
- Shop with waist-length and inseam measurements to save trying on things that are too short.
- And also thin, take advantage of textures, i.e., mohair, cashmere, Harris tweeds, etc., and have fun mixing them.

IF YOU ARE THIN:

- Blouson your blouses and dresses—don't wear slinky, skintight fabrics.
- Yokes, gathers, tucking, ruffles are great.
- Skirts with movement are more flattering than straight skirts.
- Dramatic wider belts are possible, even if you're short-waisted because you're thin.
- Vertical stripes are bad.
- No clinging jerseys.
- Sleeveless styles are most unflattering—even bare halters are better.
- In the summer, soft elbow-length sleeves are best.
- Dark stockings make legs look even thinner.
- Hide a skinny collarbone with a choker. Cover protruding chest bones with a necklace. An upper-arm bangle can relieve a too skinny bareness.
- Wear textures that add dimension and interest but are not too gutsy, because they may overwhelm.

IF YOU ARE HEAVY:

- Pretty colors and prints give you life.
- Better quality clothes look under less strain on a heavy body.
- Hems should be medium length. Too long will make you look short, too short will make your clothes look skimpy.
- And your skirt is full, fabric must be lightweight, or you will look puffed out.
- Keep one tone to your whole outfit, including stockings and shoes, to create impression of longer, slimmer line.
- Never wear anything tight, or with excess fabric. Good fit is vital.
- And overblouses look good on you, two small open side seams make for easier fit over the hips.
- No big details—epaulettes, ruffles, bows, huge sleeves, big collars.
- Don't wear your biggest piece of jewelry.
- Don't wear thick blanket wools or mohairs, and no see-through delicate fabrics.
- Good grooming in hairstyle and makeup is vital because that is where you want the focus to be.

When and how to break the rules

A very large dynamic opera singer I know has broken every rule in the book (not this book!). She is easily a size 16, and if she followed the conventional wisdom, she would live in dark colors and black. Yet her signature is color—the brighter the better. She wouldn't dream of wearing black, of giving up what gives her joy. Every time you see her, she's in a different color, a *brilliant* color—cobalt blue, poppy red, parrot green. (She changes her makeup to go with everything she wears.)

No self-effacing, medium-sized prints for this free soul. She wears clothes that make dramatic statements—clothes in keeping with that star quality she radiates. She's decided, rightly, that she wants her image to match her personality rather than her body. In choosing clothes most women would do well to take both body and soul into consideration, but in a case like this, the psyche so outshines the body, it's more than okay to break the rules. It's a must!

Another client of ours had a different kind of problem. She dressed to "hide" because she was so tall (6 feet!) and skinny, she felt she stood out jarringly in any crowd. She stuck to smooth, flat textures and undramatic silhouettes so she wouldn't call attention to herself. We showed her how to break the "rules" and break out of her self-imposed prison. "Face it," we told her, "you're always going to look outstandingly taller than anyone else. So why not accept that fact of life—and capitalize on it!"

We showed her beautiful heavy handknit sweaters to replace her bland blazers, feminine angora tops to replace her skinny silk blouses, full dramatic tweedy midi-skirts to replace her dull A-lines, and topped them with handsome new wide belts—hers to show off better than anyone because of her long slim waist.

The most important thing we aimed for was that she should always feel feminine. In these new clothes, dramatic in texture but soft in color, she never feels too tall to be feminine. And now she loves standing out!

A third client of ours learned to break a different set of rules. A size 4, only 5'1", she knew what she was supposed to do to look taller: wear one solid color head to toe and only in the simplest of lines. Today she's more sure of herself and she's accepted the fact that she's never going to be—or look—more than 5'1". She's discovered a marvelous public image. Small as she is, she has excellent proportions, so she can wear almost anything she wants after all. She's having more fun with a much more interesting image: wearing a jacket with a dramatic stand-up collar, small and medium-sized prints, mixing colors together (even bright ones), wearing the same fashions a taller woman can wear, including midi-skirts so long as they stop at the right point on *her* leg. In making her statement, she is an equal in any crowd, because the message she sends is as strong and clear as if she were 5'10".

If you're happy with yourself, that will come through in your face and manner no matter what you do.

"When it comes to clothes," one of my clients said when she first came to me, "I have two problems that never seem to go away. The gap problem: There's always one thing missing—or one outfit missing—when I need it most. And the color problem: Half of what I have doesn't go with the other half. So no matter what time of year it is, half my wardrobe is out of commission."

She is not alone. If you wish, as she does, that you could reach into your closet blindfolded, and whatever you picked would go with whatever else you picked—it's not a totally impossible dream. You can come a lot closer to it than you think, as you'll see by the year-round wardrobe itemized below. It's worked out in each of the two most common core colors—black and camel—usually preferred for the important pieces of a wardrobe. Colors and fabrics for the other pieces are chosen to give you the most variety and to go with the greatest number of other pieces. (The letters B, C, and P, after each item stand for Business, Casual, and Party [social] and indicate which of these three parts of your life the particular piece can be used for.)

Note 1. Please notice that both wardrobes have many cream or white tops. That's because they're always safe with any color combinations.

Note 2. Everywhere I say "brown," if you substitute a lighter shade—milk chocolate or cinnamon brown, say—your outfits will look more sophisticated because the contrasts still work, but are more subtle.

Note 3. Wear patterns only with solids. Mixing two patterns is tricky and calls for sophisticated understanding before it is attempted.

Either of these wardrobes will have you covered the whole year round. I've selected only one or two highlight colors, but if you have the budget for more pieces, work around three or four highlights that go with camel or black, and have a good time!

BASIC YEAR-ROUND "GOT YOU COVERED" WARDROBE IN CORE COLOR CAMEL
(WITH ACCENTS OF CINNAMON, BROWN, CREAM, TEAL BLUE)

1. *Outer Wear*
Camel wool coat (B)
Cream raincoat (B/C)
Camel outdoor jacket (B/C)
Brown/cream print shawl (B/P)

2. *Jackets*
Camel/brown/blue tweed (B/C)
Brown velvet (B/P)
Cream linen (B/P)
Blue silk (B/P)

3. *Skirts*
Brown wool (B/C)
Camel/brown tweed (B/C)
Brown/cream/blue rayon
  challis print (B/P)
Blue silk (B/P)
Cream cotton, solid (B/C)
Camel/brown/cream cotton
  floral print (B/C)

4. *Pants*
Brown wool (B/C)
Camel gabardine (B/P)
Cream silk, heavy weight (P)
Camel cotton (C)
Blue jeans (C)

5. *Blouses*
Cream cotton shirt (B/C)
Brown/cream cotton shirt,
  geometric print (B/C)
Blue silk blouse (B/P)
Cream silk or polyester
  blouse (B/P)
Camel silk or polyester
  V-neck, short sleeve blouse
  (B/C)
Brown/cream/blue challis
  blouse, floral print (B/P)

6. *Sweaters*
Cream angora (P)
Blue cotton handknit
  pullover (B/C)
Camel/cream cardigan,
  tweedy texture (B/C)

7. *Vests*
Camel wool sweater-knit (B/C)
Cream handknit cotton (B/C)

8. *Belts*
Brown tailored (B/C)
Gold metal links (B/C/P)
Cream/gold dressy (P)

9. *Shoes and Boots*
Brown pumps (B/P)
Beige, brown-toe slingback
  heels (B/P)
Cream high-heel sandals (B/P)
Brown pant shoes (B/C)
Cream summer flats (B/C)
Brown leather boots (B/C)
Brown rubber boots (B/C)

10. *Bags*
Brown shoulder bag (B/C)
Brown tailored clutch (B/P)
Brown/camel textured casual
  tote (C)
Cream dressy clutch (P)

BASIC YEAR-ROUND "GOT YOU COVERED" WARDROBE IN CORE COLOR BLACK
(WITH ACCENTS OF RED, WHITE, YELLOW)

1. **Outer Wear**
   Black wool coat (B)
   Red raincoat (B/C)
   Black outdoor jacket (C)
   Black/red/yellow print shawl (P)

2. **Jackets**
   Black/white tweed (B/C)
   Black velvet (B/P)
   White linen (B/P)
   Yellow silk (B/P)

3. **Skirts**
   Black wool (B/C)
   Black/white tweed (B/C)
   Black/white/red rayon
     challis (B/P)
   Yellow silk (B/P)
   White cotton, solid (B/C)
   Black/red/yellow cotton, floral
     print

4. **Pants**
   Black wool (B/C)
   Black gabardine light-
     weight (B/P)
   Black silk, heavy weight (P)
   White cotton (C)
   Blue jeans (C)

5. **Blouses**
   White cotton shirt (B/C)
   White/red cotton shirt,
     geometric print (B/C)
   Yellow silk (B/P)
   White silk or polyester (B/P)
   Black silk or polyester,
     V-neck short sleeves (B/C)
   Black/white/red/yellow
     challis, floral print (B/P)

6. **Sweaters**
   Yellow angora (P)
   Red cotton handknit
     pullover (B/C)
   Black/white cardigan,
     tweedy texture (B/C)

7. **Vests**
   Red wool sweater-knit (B/C)
   Yellow handknit cotton (B/C)

8. **Belts**
   Black tailored (B/C)
   Silver metal links (B/C/P)
   Red/silver dressy (P)

9. **Shoes and Boots**
   Black pumps (B/P)
   White, black-toe slingback
     heels (B/P)
   Red high-heel sandals (B/P)
   Black pant shoes (B/C)
   Red summer flats (B/C)
   Black leather boots (B/C)
   Black rubber boots (B/C)

10. **Bags**
    Black shoulder bag (B/C)
    Black tailored clutch (B/P)
    Black/white textured casual
      tote (C)
    Red dressy clutch (P)

Other wardrobe combinations to inspire your creative imagination:

CORE COLORS	YOUR CHOICE OF ACCENTS
Taupe (gray and camel combined)	Light gray/red/black
Gray	Light pink/black/rose
Navy	White/turquoise/red
Burgundy	Pale yellow/rust/dark brown
Dark green	Cherry red/cream/black

The "Formula Wardrobe"; what it is— and isn't

Perhaps you're thinking, "But isn't a 'formula wardrobe' very close to being 'in uniform'?" And haven't I warned against dressing in uniform? Indeed I have—and my warning still stands. The "formula wardrobe" is just a place to start. But it's not, I hope, where you aim to finish. That would be too modest a goal. Understanding the formula is like knowing your ABCs—you have to know them to see how they make the whole word. But you won't really know how to speak fluent clothing language if you never progress beyond them. You'll be dressing by rote—and rote won't protect you from every mistake, like a wrong mix of fabric, for instance. A case in point: Even if the colors are right, a wool or velvet jacket doesn't go with a light cotton skirt. Think of your fabrics in terms of seasons. You wouldn't mix winter with summer, but you might mix a spring weight with summer or winter, or mix a fall weight with summer or winter. (See discussion on fabrics for the different seasons on p. 78.) And make sure you don't come out looking top-heavy by wearing too heavy a fabric on top.

LITTLE LIFTS

1. Wear a pullover sweater on the outside and belt it for a change.
2. Button the last couple of buttons of your cardigan, and blouse it over a belt for a sweater-jacket look.
3. Wrap your long ties on your blouse around your neck a second time and loop them over into an ascot instead of always tying a center bow.
4. Tie a half-bow asymmetrically to the side of your blouse.
5. Twist two contrasting belts together before tying them around your waist.
6. Twist two contrasting scarves together before tying them around your neck.
7. Push up your sleeves.
8. Add a touch of needed color with a narrow velvet or grosgrain ribbon under your blouse collar.
9. Tie a sweater of interesting color contrast over your shoulders to finish your look.
10. Throw a shawl over your jacket or coat for style and drama.
11. Belt and slightly blouse your long overblouse or tunic. It's a more finished look (even if you can't see the belt!).
12. Hang a long contrasting scarf around your raincoat collar just for color interest even if you don't intend to wear it.
13. Always finish your outfit with a belt when possible even if only the buckle will show.
14. Fold over the top of your boots for a new look, or tuck your pants into your boots for a cropped pant look.
15. Put your inside collar on top of the outside collar and stand them up a little at the back of your neck.
16. A small to medium-sized fabric flower in leather or silk is a nice touch. It's usually more chic in a dark color, maroon or navy or brown. If it's bright red, it's best on a dark tailored dress or suit.
17. Keep a soft silk bowtie in your desk to turn an informal blouse into an instantly more important look.

CREATIVE FIXES

1. Buy a beautiful antique collar if you own pullover sweaters with bare jewel necklines.
2. Have a jeweler convert an unused ring or pin into a choker.
3. Change a nothing sweater or blouse by changing to wonderful old buttons.
4. Make the hem of a too-long midi-skirt into a long wide cummerbund sash for the waist.
5. Spice up a drab color with complementary bright accessories.
6. If your skirt is slightly on the short side, wearing stockings of the same tint will continue the color downward and make the skirt look longer.
7. If your shoulders are narrow or sloped, put shoulderpads in all your tops, including your blouses.
8. A blouse and different-color skirt can be turned into an "outfit" with a shawl having the same two colors in its print.
9. If your skirt or pants feel a little short, wear flat shoes.
10. Usually if you can't figure out the right shoe to wear with a skirt, boots work best.
11. If your whole outfit is chic, elegant and quiet don't jar the mood by accessorizing with a bright accent of scarf or jewelry. Keep the mood! If what you want is more a sense of fun and excitement than elegance, then experiment with contrasts, but it will probably work out better on a different outfit.
12. Keep your classic pageboy going all week long—wear a hairband by midweek as the curl starts to loosen, and turn it into a chignon with tortoise combs by weekend.

QUICK SAVES

1. If your hem comes down just before you have to go into a meeting, tape it.
2. If your stockings are splattered with mud spots and you can't change them, wash the spots off your bare skin and they'll practically disappear off your stockings. Any smudges left will also vanish if you wipe them off your stockings with a damp paper towel.

3. In rainy weather, protect hair that goes limp easily with a loose scarf rather than a hat that squooshes it down. Bring hair combs or pins to put your hair back up if you've got an important lunch to go to.

4. On menstrual days wear pretty colors and keep your makeup lively. Be extra sure to check your coloring during the day. You may need a few more applications of blusher.

SHOPPING: TREK OR TREAT? (THE CHOICE IS YOURS)

Coping with the stores

Get to know the stores in your area well enough to know which ones are for you. And which aren't. Most stores select their merchandise with a particular kind of woman in mind. When you find the stores and/or departments that most generally seem to have what you like—at the price brackets that are most comfortable for you—you can skip the rest. From that moment on, you'll automatically save a great deal of time and energy on every shopping trip.

Once you've settled on the stores you want to concentrate on, learn how to make the most of what they offer. Among the stores whose merchandise generally fits your image, one may have a particularly outstanding department in coats, while another has the best lingerie in town, and a third can't be beat for the dash and variety of their separates. Whatever you're after, before you let yourself be waited on, check out the whole range of stock first. You can't count on salespeople to do it for you. There aren't enough of them and they're too busy to give that much attention to one customer's needs. If you already know their stock, you can ask for what you want with more authority. And you'll be less likely to let the clerks intimidate you.

Never buy under pressure—no matter where it's coming from. Your husband, your best friend, your mother, the salesclerk. The time of day, the time of year, the time of sale. Because the party is next week . . . the boat sails tomorrow . . . your roommate's handsome brother is coming to town. It's hard to keep a cool head under such circumstances, and you need a cool head when you're deciding whether a particular garment is right for your body and your life over the long term. Pressure purchases seldom turn out to be lasting treasures.

Look ahead, but don't try to buy too much in advance. Tastes change and yours are likely to be constantly improving as you keep an eye on the changes in fashion.

Concentrate on getting the most important or difficult part of an outfit first. It's easier, for instance, to find a solid color skirt or pant to match with a print or plaid blouse than to find just the right print to go with a solid color skirt or pant. But if you're difficult to fit on the bottom, shop for that part first whether it's a skirt or pant and then shop for the perfect print blouse to go with it. It's a good idea to check out several stores the day before you plan to buy, so you won't feel you might be missing out on a better bet somewhere else. Don't take the word of salespeople. They can't be objective when their overriding concern is to make the sale.

When you've decided you really want to buy a particular item, check it over carefully for flaws. It's such a disappointment to discover something wrong after you've brought it home—and particularly when you have to spend time and energy you can't spare to take it back. But if you really love it, don't give up too easily. If there's only one left in your size, and it's the perfect top to match your favorite skirt, and the flaw is a rip in the seam that you could stitch yourself—take it. Don't count on the store to fix it. All they'll do is send it back to the manufacturer. Very few stores will special order another one or repair it or help you find a substitute. And you know how long it took you to find the original.

Be sure to ask about the store's return policy before you walk out with your find of the week. The skirt you thought would work beautifully with your tweed jacket might turn out to be just two shades off the mark when you get it home under normal light. Just to be on the safe side, take the name and extension of the sales clerk. When you add up how much time and annoyance—and expense— can be wasted on returning things, it pays to spend a little extra time when you're shopping to avoid all that.

Saving time   When you're a working woman, saving time when you shop may be more important—and more profitable—than saving money. I've said it before but it's worth repeating, knowing your image is one of

106

the best time-savers, because it narrows down the stores you shop in. You don't waste precious lunch hours or Thursday nights wandering around foreign—and barren—territory.

The second most obvious time-saver is to shop when the clothes are *there*. That means shopping in August for fall-winter, in March for spring-summer. That's when the merchandise is in full supply, when there are no gaps in sizes and colors and coordinates. And if you're one of those women who find it hard to psych themselves up for fur-lined coats and cashmere in 90° August heat or bathing suits and gauzy Indian cotton in the chill winds of March, think how smug you'll feel to have your wardrobe all together *ahead* of time. And how much more fun it will be to spend the next few months enjoying the season *wearing* the clothes, instead of using up the season shopping for them.

Check over what you have before you go shopping. If you're trying to match something you already have, bring the "something" along. It may seem like a bother, but it's actually a Grade A time and energy saver. Saves you all those five and ten minute chunks of pondering and wondering and trying to see it in your mind's eye— colors are the hardest things in the world to "remember"—and it does away with return trips. Cutting a snip from a seam to match color sometimes isn't enough. You need the whole garment there to get the balance of texture and color. Sometimes a perfect match isn't "perfect." The texture may be too bland, the outfit boring.

Wear or bring flattering shoes for trying on new looks. The dress that looked just right for you on the hanger may look disappointingly wrong on you, if you're trying to assess its impact in your clunky low-heeled walking shoes.

Even if you're shopping for one specific thing, a smoky blue blouse for example, keep your eyes open for a great find. The smoky blue blouse may just not be there that day, but it isn't a wasted shopping trip if you come back with something else you also need, but didn't have down as your target of the day—a string vest that will make many outfits.

If you don't have the money to snap things up when you see them, you'll probably have to spend more time pulling your look together. It takes longer to find that sweater that goes beautifully with three skirts than with just one. Many of our clients, after several seasons of shopping with us, are amazed at how that sweater we bought for one particular skirt seems, almost magically, to go with many other bottoms we bought in past seasons. It's a simple secret—there's a consistency of taste and image that makes each part "go"—no matter how far apart in time the items were bought.

Saving money
There are three basic ways to save money when you buy clothes: shopping "mechanics," shopping principles, shopping "tricks." Any one of them can make a happy difference in your clothes costs, but if you learn and use all three, you'll be amazed at how terrific you can look for how little.

*Sorting out
the sales*
Shopping "mechanics" are, of course, buying things on sale. It pays to know what kinds of sales stores run and the various times of the year they run them.

KINDS OF SALES

- Regular merchandise marked down.
- "Special purchase"—good buy by store for sale. Usually items the manufacturer couldn't sell at the regular price.
- Clearance sale—items kicking around too long. Sold "as is" so examine carefully for flaws.
- Comparable value—just an advertising term. Store feels the $20 item it has is comparable to a $40 item elsewhere.
- Liquidation sale—store going out of business. Ask yourself why merchandise wasn't good enough to keep the store in business.
- Irregulars—make sure you know what "irregular" is and whether the item is worth buying, even at the reduced price.

The three major markdown periods are after Christmas, after Easter, after July 4. Columbus Day and Washington's birthday are also big days.

Shopping principles
The shopping *principles* of saving money are few—but powerful and far-reaching. The first is: Invest in a trend, not in a fad. Trends come on relatively slowly, evolve and mature over a period of time,

and fade gently and gradually. Fads, however, often seem to spring up in a day, a week, or a month, saturate the marketplace, and vanish overnight. A trend is a longer-length fuller skirt. A fad is a split skirt or satin culottes for evening.

	TRENDY	FADDY
1.	Leather and suede	Metallic leather
2.	Longer, fuller skirts	Culotte slit skirts
3.	Wide belts	Lace-up waist-cinchers
4.	Authentic ethnic accessories	Metallic corded jewelry
5.	Flatter heels	Ballet slippers
6.	Metallic glimmers	Camouflage jungle prints
7.	Authentic antique blouses	Peasant blouses
8.	Jumpsuits	Overalls
9.	Shorter jackets	Bolero jackets
10.	Large shawls	Ponchos
11.	Capes	Blanket throws
12.	Shoulder pads	Ruffle-edged overextended shoulder pads

Invest in a trend, not a fad

If you get good at detecting trends as they start to gather momentum, you'll always look right in fashion, without spending a lot of money. If you fall for fads, you'll waste money two ways. The faddish thing you buy will look out of date the next season, before you get your money's worth out of it. And you'll find yourself having to spend money on the next fad, so you won't feel out of fashion.

Buy all-season clothes

The second shopping principle is to make as many of your purchases as possible all-season clothes. And use different accessories to make the outfits look "seasonal." Buy a skirt or dress in corduroy, gabardine, or lightweight wool—good for at least nine months of the year. In the spring, accessorize it with luggage (caramel) shoes, a straw bag, and a pastel print scarf. Choose a burgundy suede boot, burgundy leather bag, add a sweater vest, and you can wear the same skirt or dress right through fall and winter.

One of the commonest mistakes I've seen clients make is to have two distinctly different wardrobes for spring-summer and fall-winter. Different colors, short-season fabrics make each set good for only half the year, thereby making each wardrobe look unnecessarily skimpy, when with a little planning and more careful choices, the clothes could work the year round and appear to double the size of your wardrobe.

Figure cost
per wearing

A third money-saving principle is to calculate the cost of an item not by the price tag, but by the *cost per wearing*. A $100 dress you wear twice a year is an extravagance. A $300 jacket and skirt you wear different ways six times a month is a smart buy and more affordable than you think. It's hard to break out of your self-built prison, but when you judge too strictly by the price tag of a garment, you're imprisoning yourself unnecessarily. It's not only bad wardrobe planning—it's bad money management. Stretch your budget as far as you can to make sure the clothes you wear most often will be of the best quality. But be ruthless when it comes to spending *any* money—whether it's $5 or $50 or $100—for something you feel you won't be seen in more than once or twice.

Smart finds
in offbeat places

LOOK IN THE GIRLS' DEPARTMENT . . .

for a cape—her long might be your midi
for tennis clothes
for boots
for dickeys and collars
for ribbed knee socks

LOOK IN THE JUNIOR DEPARTMENT . . .

for T-shirts (you don't have to be small, you can be a size 13)
for nightgowns and robes
for camisoles
for casual fun or sport clothes

110

LOOK IN THE BOYS AND YOUNG MEN'S DEPARTMENT . . .

for pea jackets and down vests
for denim work shirts
for a ruffled tuxedo shirt as a smashing blouse
for a navy blazer
for sweater vests
for an argyle pullover sweater
for rain slickers

AND TRY . . .

evening wear possibilities in Lingerie and At Home departments
a knockout costume jewelry pin on a suede sash for a belt buckle
buying shoulder pads separately, for last year's blouses

Shopping "tricks" are the third good way to save money. When *Shopping "tricks"* maillot one-piece bathing suits are in, buy a Danskin body suit for $14. Instead of getting a silk shawl in the shawl department for a summer evening wrap, get a cotton open-weave shawl from the beachwear department. Pick up a loose sundress in the junior dress department. If it's not long enough for flair, get a floor-length one and cut it to midi-length. Save money on accessories—shop the junior floor for summer jewelry. (Shop junior coats and separates whenever possible.) Choose a nice straw bag and it will look as right with an evening gown as with sports clothes. And its natural texture goes with every color.

Borrow one of the smartest tricks of all from savvy European women. Class up a whole inexpensive outfit or wardrobe with one really expensive item. Throwing your last $180 into a tweed riding jacket may be one of the thriftiest buys you ever made. It will give that indefinable touch of class to everything you wear with it.

And the best way to save money and time together is to buy a good basic when you see it. An off-white silk shirt, a small colored kerchief—something you know you're going to need, know you can always use, and never have too many of. When you find it at a good price, buy it even if you don't need it at that very minute. You will.

You can improve your shopping results noticeably if you train

111

yourself to ask these questions automatically, when you're at the crucial deciding point: *To Buy or Not to Buy*.

Do I *need* this item? If not, can I afford to buy it just because I want it?
Is it worth the thrill?
Is it flattering? Is it the image I want to present?
Does the color go with my coloring and other things I plan to wear with it?
Is it comfortable?
Am I willing to put up with the upkeep?
If it costs more than I should spend, but I love it, can I use it for double-duty in any way?

Shopping smart   SAVING TIME

Remember which manufacturers make clothes that fit you without alterations.
Make one salesperson yours—and ask her to call you for mark-downs. Or call her to inquire.

SAVING MONEY

Whatever you don't need immediately, save shopping for until you can hit the sales.
Send your purchases to a friend in a nontaxable area if you're planning to see her in the near future.
Buy skirts with deep hems so they can be lengthened.

NEVER BUY . . .

Anything extremely tight, extremely short, extremely anything.
Anything to grow into or reduce down to!
Anything if you've just gained or lost weight. Wait till you level off.
Fragile fabrics for work.
Skirts with large border designs on hems. Lengths may change and you'll be stuck with a big alteration or an impossible one.
Light-colored suedes—they're exorbitantly expensive to clean.

112

If you're on a budget, buy the latest *accessory* rather than the latest in clothing.

Buy adjustable belts or sashes if your waist fluctuates.

Buy your basic hose on sale—twelve pairs for $25.

Buy medium to dark-colored boots, just as you'd buy a medium-to-dark rug that's going to get use.

Buy as many machine-washable or hand-washable garments as possible, if they are good-looking.

Keep accessories in three families of colors and moods: two different colors that are practical yet different for work, and one more interesting for intrigue and fun.

If you don't love it, you must need it badly—or else don't get it!

CLOSETS: LAW AND ORDER—OR CRIMINAL NEGLIGENCE?

Few things you do for yourself will pay off as immediately—and handsomely—as getting your closets in good working order. Conversely, few things can trip you up more often, or slow you down so constantly, or feed a bad self-image so much as closets *not* in good working order. Jumbled closets are as big an energy-waster as jumbled files in the office and can lead to equally embarrassing crises.

How good your closet is has very little to do with how big it is . . . how up-to-the-minute the decor is . . . or how many matching gadgets and accessories it has. Whether your closets rate an A or an F depends on the answers to three absurdly simple questions. Is there enough room for everything you keep in it? Is everything easily seen? Is everything easy to get at?

If all three answers are yes, you can skip this section. If any—or all—are no, read on.

Finding space

The first alibi all closet-flunkers come up with is the classic "I just don't have enough space." As alibis go, it's not bad. In today's small houses and apartments, with today's living arrangements with grabby roommates or husbands who are bigger than you are, it sounds like simple truth to say, "I just don't have the space."

But the simple truth *is* there's lots more space than meets the eye—especially if your eye hasn't been looking in the right place. The right place—unless you live alone—may well be over the negotiating table with your roommate or husband, especially if the two of you have been trying to share a single closet. People you love dearly can infringe on your territory without even noticing. If you've been thinking we're dividing "even-Steven," and they've been thinking we're dividing "roughly even," you both may find you're not nearly as close as you thought. Hammer it all out or horse-trade if you have to, "I'll give you X amount of my drawer space for your shirts, if I can have X more hanger space for my blouses." But get the space fairly divided—and clearly understood.

Making space

Next, in the space that's really, truly yours—and still really, truly not enough—where do you find more space? Right on the hangers. All those hangers with out-of-season clothes: Get them out. All those hangers with evening clothes and coats: Get them out. (They stand alone, so they don't need to be with your other clothes.) All those hangers with clothes that fit you ten pounds ago, clothes you love but haven't had a chance to wear in a year, "mistake" clothes you wish you'd never bought and haven't had the courage to give away. Clothes in all these categories can go in closets of other rooms, can be packed away in suitcases you're not using, or held in storage by your friendly neighborhood cleaner.

Conquering space

If you've done your "weeding" thoroughly, every item in your closet will be something you're currently wearing, currently happy with. Every item will be hanging unsquooshed (hence unwrinkled), easy to pull out without tugging. And no item you're currently wearing will be lost in the back of the closet or out of sight, out of mind, in a drawer or a box on a shelf. You'll have a bird's-eye view of your whole wardrobe every time you open the closet door. And you won't be lulled into thinking you've got lots of clothes when you haven't because so many unwearables are mixed in with the wearables. (A fact you're likely to discover only when you try to pull an outfit together.)

What goes where— and why

Now—two simple divisions of hanger space will make your closet even more efficient. Clothes for work in one section (group all jackets together, all skirts, pants, blouses, then all third-layer items, vests and tunics). Clothes only for home and fun in the next section. (You should, of course, take a tweed jacket from your work section and integrate it with jeans for a weekend.) Clothes needing fix-up go on a hook on the closet wall. (Fix-up can be anything from a trip to the cleaners, to a sagging hem, a missing button, a stain that needs pre-treating. Any item you can't wear again until it's "fixed" goes here.)

You can mark the divisions with an empty different-color hanger, or a hanger with an empty plastic bag on it. If you want to keep your newly all-in-order closet really orderly, buy a decorator coatrack to stash things on. Put tomorrow's outfit on this, along with the clothes you wore that day to air out before they go back into the closet.

All storage space in your closet should be see-through. It's a waste of energy and a threat to your normally good disposition to have to unzip zippers, uncover boxes, etc., to find what you're looking for. Out of sight is not only hard to find, but also hard to remember, so don't put things in drawers if you can hang them in the closet. Even some knit dresses are better off over a padded hanger where you can see them than in a drawer where they're easy to forget.

Hang belts by color or category (ethnic, evening, sporty, etc.) close to clothes. Shoes should be on a rack close to a full-length mirror, so it's easy to try on several pairs before you decide which goes best with the outfit you're planning to wear. Evening bags and interesting straw totes can be hung on the wall too—you'll "create" precious storage space and add a little zip to your decor. Shawls look great on the wall. Put sweaters on open shelves on top of the closet. Have a separate dresser tray for your watch, jewelry, etc., and keep the things you use most often in the easiest drawer to pull out.

In sum, you'll run your life better—and show it—if you keep your closet, like your car, in good running order. Give it an overhaul every six months—*before* the next season starts. When all the parts of your wardrobe are checked over and in gear, it should take you everywhere in style!

6

THE UNDERSIDE OF GETTING AHEAD . . .
Keeping Ahead

Getting your image and wardrobe together is the first thing to do as a working woman because it makes everything else easier. It's the quickest, most effective way to start things changing—in *your* favor.

When you look good, you feel good. When you feel good, you do better. When you do better, you get more competent, more confident, readier to take on new challenges, go for bigger prizes.

But image can't do it all. In teaching my clients how important image and clothing language are in getting ahead on the job, I've learned with them—and from them—the importance of the underside of that task: keeping ahead *off* the job by organizing your life. And that's the next priority to tackle, because lack of organization is the other major liability that keeps us at less than our best.

If there's one thing we all have in common—we women who work—it's the pressure of time. Whether we're married or single, with children or without, well up on the corporate ladder or just starting the climb, the one thing we all don't have is time. *Enough time.*

And never having enough time can undermine self-confidence as surely, steadily, and disastrously as never having the right clothes. It sends all the wrong messages about us to others—and to ourselves.

116

We haven't got things under control. We don't manage things well. We don't have our priorities straight. We don't have enough discipline. We don't have the right sense of ourselves. We haven't understood that time is Money. And more crucial even than that, time is Life. It's our life we're missing when we don't have enough time to do what we want, as well as we want, at the time we want to, and should, do it. And the reason so many of us are in this boat—permanently, it often seems—is again that old basic, "not enough time." And we don't take the time to figure out a better way to organize ourselves and our families.

Since you're taking the time to read this book, you're already taking the first step down a different road. A road to lead you to every working woman's dream of buried treasure—*all kinds of time*. "Me" time. "Us" time. Put-your-feet-up time. Read-a-book-without-guilt time. Play-with-the-baby time. Loll-in-the-tub time. Saturday-afternoon-antiquing time. Writing-a-long-letter-home time. Staring-into-space-don't-have-to-do-a-damn-thing time!

It's these little cushions of time that keep the bounce in our lives. Keep us feeling human and happy and proud of our ability to cope. We've all known periods when our lives are so jammed there's no room for these little lifesavers for days or even weeks. But if we go too long without them, the ill effects show up all too soon. It's like living too long on junk food—sooner or later you're going to come down with something. Without these little luxuries of time—not luxuries, *necessities*—you're going to come down with the blues . . . the jitters . . . and a long-term case of the drudges.

Feeling time-poor is just as grinding as feeling money-poor. The difference being, everybody starts out with the same amount of time—168 hours a week. It's how you manage it that leaves you feeling poor—or rich.

In the sections to come, I've put down the tested strategies that have worked for me and many of my clients. The little changes in action that make the big difference. The big changes in attitude that add up to a whole new kind of freedom.

ORGANIZING YOURSELF (IT'S POSSIBLE!)

The secret of survival: Energy

The secret of survival for a working woman in the '80s is going to be, quite simply, a matter of energy: How much energy she has . . . how well she conserves it . . . how wisely she spends it . . . and where she can lay her hands on more when she needs it.

Working women come in all shapes, sizes—and energy levels. Just as you can do something about your size and shape if you want to improve them, you can do something about your level of energy too. It's all a matter of attitude.

Getting rid of guilt

The first thing to do is get rid of guilt. Whether you work because you want to or because you have to, there is nothing to feel guilty about. You are not shortchanging your family. You are not aggrandizing yourself at their expense. You are not putting pride of paycheck ahead pride of progeny or the delights of eating out ahead of the duties of cooking in.

You are, in fact, looking out for the best interests of your husband and children in trying to do what you want to do. Because when *you* function best, the whole family is better off. As Nancy puts it, "I'm a better wife and mother because I work. I'm doing everything and getting nurtured by it. When it's over, I then have much more to give them."

Happiness is catching

Given a choice most families would rather eat pizza with a happy woman who forgot to thaw the roast for dinner than feast on standing ribs of beef presided over by a pursed-mouth martyr who's done what she's supposed to do—and hated every minute of it. Of course if you forgot to thaw the meat three times in one week, smiling a lot won't quite make up for it. Something in your setup needs fixing.

Like too many women, you may think there's no way of escaping guilt when you work. But if you think about it, it isn't *work* that makes you feel guilty, it's *incompetence*.

If you thought you were doing a great job at work and romancing your husband beyond his wildest dreams and putting Band-Aids on skinned knees and running up Halloween costumes for your children, it would be hard to feel guilty. It's when you can't seem to do all

118

those things at once that guilt settles like a lead weight on your shoulders.

You can shuck guilt off with a two-pronged attack. First, organize yourself better. Second, examine that word "incompetence." We are all incompetent at something. The trick is to *choose your area* of incompetence . . . and your *level* of incompetence. When it's a free choice instead of something thrust upon you by someone else, it's amazing how easily guilt can be made to disappear.

Choose your level of incompetence

Very few women feel guilty because they are incompetent at tennis, compared to Chris Evert Lloyd, say. Tennis is not their thing. Cooking may not be *your* thing. Ah, but cooking is different, you will say. It affects my husband and children. They have a right to eat well, to count on good meals, nutritionally balanced, and on time.

So they do. But not necessarily meals that take an hour or more to make . . . meals that outshine those on the glossy pages of the women's magazines . . . meals that call for endless peeling and chopping and browning and basting and baking . . . meals that only *your* two hands can make. The alternative need not be a dreary succession of fast food and deli takeout.

It is entirely possible to put together a private recipe file of meals and menus that take no more than half an hour from the time you step into the kitchen to when the family sits down at the table. (And this does not mean steak and hamburgers five times a week.) It is entirely possible to have meals in the freezer that your husband and children can heat up themselves if you are stuck in a late meeting at work. It is entirely possible to make long-cooking casseroles and roasts on the weekend that you can feast on for days through the week. It is even possible to train each member of the family (ten years or older) to be able to make one meal that will see them through when you are unavoidably absent. (Just make sure the necessary ingredients are always on hand.) If the Boy Scouts can do it, they can too. And they'll feel proud of themselves besides!

Cooking is only one area where a little serious thought in advance can lead to a great easing of pressure long-term. The overriding principle is to set things up to be as easy as possible for yourself. Not because you're selfish or lazy, but because that's the way you'll have more to give your family, your job—and even yourself.

119

The rule of   You can do it with the rule of the four Ds: Don't do it. Do it now.
the 4 Ds   Do it fast. Do it easy.

Sit down with a pad and pencil and make a quick list of just what you do and have in your life and your work. Ask if you do it or have it because you want it . . . because people expect it . . . because you've always done it . . . because you've never really thought about it. Consider what it takes to have it, or do it, and ask if it's worth it. And you may come up with a list that falls under the heading . . .

Don't do it   1. Don't make a hot meal from scratch seven nights a week.
2. Don't cater to each person's favorite food in the same meal.
3. Don't get trapped into a different mealtime for different members of the family.
4. Don't clean up your child's room or your husband's closet.
5. Don't collect everyone's dirty laundry from their drawers and closets and floors. Each member should put his dirty laundry (including unballed socks) into the basket for whites or the one for colors.
6. Don't buy clothes that need careful handwashing or ironing if your help or you are terrible at it.
7. Don't have a lot of plants and pets at home when you're too busy to keep them all alive and happy.
8. Don't bleach your floors to a fashionable light color if you don't have someone to wax them regularly.
9. Don't get light carpeting if you have to worry about traffic. Even industrial carpeting doesn't last three years if it's light.
10. Don't write long guilt-ridden letters to your mother. Frequent short postcards or telephone calls are better.
11. Don't get involved in conflicting plans involving others. Keep life schedules simple.

While your "Don't do it" list can be a lot longer than you think when you start, you will eventually have to come to grips with the "Do it" lists. The first of which is *Do It Now*. What belongs on this list is anything that will take twice as long if you do it later.

Do it now—and think of all the free time that will pile up because you don't have to think about it again . . . won't have to arrange to do it . . . won't have to waste time berating yourself for not having done it . . . won't have to apologize to somebody else for being late doing it.

Do it now means wipe it up now . . . put it away now. Hang it up now . . . wash the dishes now . . . get rid of it now. Not because your mother told you (though she probably did), but because after it's hardened it'll take more than a wipe . . . after you've left it there, it'll disappear . . . after you've dropped it on the chair, you'll have to iron it . . . after you've left the dishes, there are no dishes left, or counter space, or room in the sink . . . after you've saved it for three weeks, you'll still have to get rid of it.

"I've given up next-morning thank-you phone calls," says my friend Dee. "I write two-sentence thank you notes to my hostess instead." She's right. It saves you the four telephone calls you have to make before you reach her: the line's busy, she's out, wrong number, that phone machine again. It saves getting caught up in a fifteen-minute conversation when you do reach her. And it makes her feel good—a personal compliment and appreciation among all those depressing bills and junk mail.

Do it fast . . . or at least faster. This doesn't mean you have to speed up till you look like an escapee from the assembly line of a Chaplin movie. There's nothing worse than feeling "out of breath" psychologically because you're always in a hurry. Though everyone has her own natural optimal rhythm, your pace on routine tasks may be more a matter of habit, or simple unawareness, than inability to do it faster.

"When I was single I remember spending two hours on myself just to go out," says Marian. "Now I do it in fifteen to twenty minutes. Looking forward to going out is like a shot of adrenaline."

Next time you're in the supermarket, notice the pace of the checkout girls. A practiced few get your order bagged in a blink, others look as if they're doing it in slow motion. Same thing at the post office, the bank, the ticket office at the theater, etc.

Never underestimate the thrill of beating the system. When a job is basically boring, it's understandable that you may not approach it

Do it now

Do it fast

121

with verve and spirit, but if you let your boredom set the pace, you'll cheat yourself of the time you'd have to yourself if you did the job at maximum speed and got it over with. Stepping up your pace not only gives you a bonus of time, but keeps you "in tone" psychologically, fends off mental flabbiness, and makes you feel good about yourself. Sometimes, it can lead to even bigger rewards. As, for instance, the story one of my clients told me.

Out of college just a year, she had left her typist job for a much better job with the government only to find, on arrival, that it had fallen through. She turned to her college placement office for emergency help and took the job they found her that very day—as a "book searcher" at Harvard's Widener Library. The work was checking card catalogs all day to see if the daily list of new books the library was thinking of buying had already been bought so they wouldn't waste money buying duplicates.

After her first few days on the job, she asked around and discovered that her co-workers usually searched an average of eighteen books an hour. Her normal output was over thirty-five. She decided to make a game of improving that score.

When she reached forty books an hour, comfortably, she worked all morning—and in the afternoon disappeared into the famed Widener "stacks," to gorge herself on a banquet of books she would never otherwise have had access to, or time for. She did this for a whole year and felt it was the equivalent of getting an extra year of college free.

No one ever asked her where she was in the afternoons—all searchers had reason to enter the stacks to check on a book from time to time—and she kept her spot as the most productive worker in the department. At the end of the year, she was asked by her boss if she would consider becoming a professional librarian. They thought she had great promise. "A job so boring it would have driven me crazy in a week," she said, "turned out to give me one of the best years of my life."

One important secret of "doing it fast" is getting whatever "it" is down to a routine. If you have certain chores you have to do every day, and you do them a little differently every time, you're wasting more time and energy than you may realize. It's worthwhile to take the time to analyze how you do even the lowliest household chore, see how well you can streamline it, and do it that way ever after.

One client told me a certain favorite family recipe that used to take forty-five minutes in preparation now takes her only fifteen, because she's done it so often she could do it in her sleep.

The second important secret of "doing it fast" is setting up your environment so it helps you do it efficiently. Just as well-set-up files in the office makes work easier—whether you're boss or secretary—setting up your environment right can also make a big difference in your productivity. Two cases in point:

Anne had always felt herself a misfit in the kitchen, because, try as she would, she could never finish cleaning up in less than forty-five minutes after a normal family meal. She had tried to speed up without success and decided that was what you got for having four children under seven.

Then came the summer they rented a new ranch house at the beach. And the kitchen cleanup that took forty-five minutes at home took only fifteen minutes here. The kitchen layout was like operating a console. You stood in the middle and everything you needed was within arm's reach—the sink, the stove, the refrigerator, the staple shelves. The only walking you had to do was to the dining table.

At home, in their big old Victorian house with that big old Victorian kitchen, you had to walk a mile to make a cup of coffee. The dishes were in the butler's pantry. The range was in the kitchen, the coffee was in the cold pantry. Everything was 20 feet from everything else and she ran everywhere she went.

"Even if you think running's good for you," she says now, "wasting half an hour on kitchen cleanup that you could be spending with your family or on yourself is a criminal waste. Even worse, it not only wastes your time and energy, it feeds your low opinion of yourself, because you can't help feeling if you were really competent you wouldn't be behind in everything all the time."

Setting up the environment right proved itself for Margaret too. For her newly-opened store of potpourri scents, she had to compile various publicity printouts to send to magazines and newspapers. Each packet of information was to be different and the papers and samples of potpourri she needed were all over the house.

Her first smart decision was to get the job done in one day. Next, she set up a card table in a corner of the den so she could spread out all the publicity sheets in the order she wanted to clip them together. Under the card table, she set three baskets filled with the three packaged scents ready for mailing. By her elbow was the name and address list of who got which so she didn't have to hunt up each magazine and newspaper editor's name. Getting organized was tedious—it took a whole day in advance—but when she finally sat down to send the material out, the job went without a hitch. It was not a long, drawn-out frustrating experience because she didn't have the right size envelopes, or she'd failed to find out who the new decorating editor was on the newspaper, or she couldn't check whether she'd actually sent one editor a different publicity piece than she sent to a competitive editor. Each name, together with what was to be sent off, was checked off so there were no slip-ups. End result? A great feeling of accomplishment.

Do it easy   When you're a working woman you simply don't have time to do things the hard way. Figuring out the easy way is not a cop-out or a surrender to sloppiness. It's making the best use of your resources, conserving energy, and being on top of things—all highly prized talents in the business world as you know. And they're every bit as profitable in your personal world.

"I've got a little list." That's the big secret of getting things under control. Have a little list of what you have to do for the week and for the day. If you're like me, knowing what you have to do is less frightening than imagining it. I like to plot the week coming up on Friday afternoons. It's the end of my working week, and the list is its punctuation. Some of my friends like Sunday night better. "When I'm thinking 'Thank God it's Friday,'" one of my clients said, "I'm not up to making lists. At the end of the weekend, when I've had my fun, I can face it with more nerve and verve."

Choose the time that's best for you—but make a list. (Preferably on one large pad, not a lot of little slips of paper.) It takes so little time that you can do it almost anywhere. On the train coming home from work. In the morning at the coffee shop. While your husband's getting ready for bed. (Have a pad and pencil on your night table.) It will give you the total picture. It will help you put things in order of importance. It will get things off your mind. And it will give you a great sense of satisfaction to cross things out as you do them.

Break the drudge work up into little pieces—so you can do them in little pieces of time. You want to save the big pieces of time for relaxing and/or enjoying the family. Household chores that can take a couple of hours if you do them the conventional housewife way can get done in a series of little five-minute attacks if you break them up.

Break up the drudge work

You don't know where you're going to find time to clean the refrigerator this week, for instance. Here's where: if you're through making the salad, while your husband is still browning the chops, clean out the vegetable crisper. If there's five minutes to go for the scalloped potatoes to come out of the oven, use the five minutes to clear all the overage leftovers out of the refrigerator. If you're waiting for the water to boil for the string beans, wrap up the meat in the meat compartment for the freezer. (Yes, you should have done it when you came home from the store with it, but you didn't have the time then, and you do have time now.) Pour yourself the last glass of cranberry juice and throw away the bottle. Pour your husband the last of the V-8 he loves and get rid of that bottle. Suddenly the shelves look surprisingly tidy and quite unjumbled. If you have to leave scrubbing them for another time, you don't feel quite so guilty. And when you're putting food away after dinner, you can wipe off the smudges on the refrigerator door at the end.

If you did this on a Saturday morning, it would take you an hour and a half. Because that would be now-we-have-to-clean-the-refrigerator day. Yet here you are with a refrigerator you wouldn't be ashamed to have your mother-in-law look into—and you did it in "no time." With a free Saturday morning to take the kids to the beach.

Irene volunteered to be responsible for the fall issue of her child's school newspaper. Each week she would review what had to be done, i.e., call Mary to write a piece on the bazaar, get three volunteers to distribute the newspapers, line the illustrator up. Anytime her children were out of the house or peacefully playing she would work her way down this list. She kept at it so diligently, the fact that she didn't have large chunks of time to give to the paper didn't matter and it all got done with ease.

You can use the divide-and-conquer technique in dozens of ways, not only to cut your household chores down to a happy minimum,

Divide and conquer

125

but to get you over the psychological block of not wanting to do the job at all. If, for instance, you don't really feel like cleaning the livingroom—hauling out the vacuum, polishing the furniture, dusting the lampshades, etc.—just do the fast preliminaries. Sort the magazines, pick up the papers, clear out the mail basket, throw out the dead flowers. Dusting, polishing, and vacuuming can wait for when you feel more like it. And in the meantime, the whole place looks a lot better than you expected. Even better, when you do get down to polishing, vacuuming, and so forth, you'll get through it in half the time.

Consolidate and conquer

Odd as it may seem—after I've just said break up the big jobs into little ones—consolidate and conquer is not a contradiction. It's the other half of getting chores under control. Don't waste time and energy doing one little thing at a time.

Don't ever make a trip to the supermarket or drugstore for just one item unless it's an emergency. Keep a bulletin board on the kitchen wall to jot down what you've run out of, at the time you've run out, and train the family to do the same. Especially if they're the type that complain when they're out of their favorite soap.

Don't pay one or two bills each day or write letters and notes at random. Save all the paper work for one day a week. You'll do it much faster and cleaner and you won't have to keep in your head what's still left to do.

Group other small chores the same way—washing pantyhose, sewing buttons and hems, etc.—so you can get rid of them painlessly while listening to music.

Never do nothing

"Don't just stand there—do something." Perhaps the most basic rule of all, and one most of us overlook too often. Never do nothing while you wait. (Never wait, if you can possibly avoid it—but if you're stuck, do *something* with the time.) At the bank or supermarket, write the check while you wait in line. If you've finished the paper on the train home, write your list of "must-dos" for the next day. If you're waiting for your child at the dentist's office, draft the letter you'll type later querying Bloomingdale's about your bill.

The idea here is not to cram every second so full you feel like a mechanical rabbit barely one hop ahead of the hounds. It's to do necessary chores in "wasted time" so you won't even feel as if you have worked. And you'll have glorious chunks to "waste" in more delightful ways.

EASY-DOES-ITS

1. When you've got a page of phone numbers and notes for calls to make, cross them out as you do them, so you won't have to reread the whole page every time you're ready to make another call.
2. Call your doctor's office to find out if he's running on schedule, so you won't have to waste time waiting for your appointment.
3. Date your hairdresser for the first appointment in the morning so you won't be hung up if there's a logjam in his schedule. Or make an evening appointment—most good salons stay open late at least one night a week.
4. Answer a phone call when it comes if you possibly can—calling back wastes time. You might be calling each other's phone machines for weeks!
5. Make your calendar your bible. Put down everything you have to do, even reminders of something that has to be done a week later. Better to put down when you should *start* something—rather than the date it's due.
6. Review your schedule constantly to see if you can cancel an unimportant appointment, or postpone it to a time when you'll be in the area for something else, a way to gain extra time in a packed day.
7. Don't do things too far ahead of time—especially if there's a chance other events could affect them. Better to bone up on your speech an hour before you're going to give it than to look it over with half an eye days ahead.
8. Don't be compulsive about keeping files. It's rarely worth the time, space, and effort involved. We forget what we have anyway, so it's never there when we need it.
9. Keep only records that will help you in the future—the rest only indicate insecurity, show your attention is focused on the past.
10. Call to let someone know you're on your way or to reconfirm a future date. If you wait till that morning you may not be able to reach her—uncertainty is tension-producing.

11. As soon as a bulb blows or a hook breaks, add it to the "to buy" list you carry with you, so you'll remember to get it when you're passing the right store.
12. Leave your office at an odd hour to avoid lines when you have to cash a check.
13. Call in your supermarket order so it can be delivered without your having to go shopping.

HOW TO SPEND ENERGY WISELY

Whether you're aware of it or not—and most women probably aren't—one of the biggest energy drains in your life is likely to be *other people*. What they expect of you, legitimately or not. How they make you feel. The problems they want to saddle you with. The roles they want you to play. You can find your reserves dangerously low . . . feel you're always running in the red, if you don't come to understand where and when to draw the line—for their sake as well as yours.

Learn to say "no"   The first thing is to learn to say no. Women have traditionally been raised to say yes except to one request—and that was a generation ago. Today most of us still find it hard to say no, even when we know saying yes is going to get us nothing but trouble.

"Yes, I'll collect for cancer the third Saturday in April. Yes, I'll take the Brownie troop on the spring overnight. Yes, I'll type your term paper for you. Yes, I'll take the car down for a tune-up. Yes, I'll return the sweater you bought to Saks. Yes, we'll invite the Bowens for dinner next Friday if you want. Yes, I'll research that project."

The more you say yes, the more things you'll be asked to say yes to—and the less time and energy you'll have for the things you really want to, have to, or should, do. And those yeses will not only be depleting your energy reserves, they'll be fostering all sorts of bad things in other people—weakening their initiative and independence . . . stunting their sense of responsibility, their ability to learn, their

128

own generosity of spirit. In a word, spoiling them rotten. And that is doing them no favor.

"My mistake was doing it all myself when I was home," says Gail. "Saying yes to everything—just to keep the peace and calm. Now that I'm working and I need that help and support, I don't think I can depend on Bill. I don't think he's capable. It might be that he hasn't been forced to. I'm not about to have a breakdown to test him."

Steel yourself to say no, and life will automatically simplify—so when you do say yes, you can do it gladly, ungrudgingly, feeling better about yourself.

Don't let them transfer their pressures to you. Don't let someone else's bad mood put a damper on your good spirits. If he or she is having an "I'm mad at the world" day . . . or sulking in his/her tent . . . or just being generally impossible, don't assume it's anything you did, or anything you should do something about. Speak softly—and give them a wide berth.

Try not to let other people get you down

A little distance—physical and psychological—does wonders at keeping you from catching whatever it is that's going around, so to speak.

Right here is a good place to point out one of the most important advantages of having a job to go to—it gets you out of the house and forces you to leave home problems at home. Yes, they may be waiting for you when you return. And then again, they may not. Even if they are, you've had a chance to get away from them for eight hours and replenish your energy reserves to meet them with. You may even see them a little differently because you've been away from them for a day. Chances are, they won't look nearly as big in the evening as they did in the morning. The wailing child you shut the door on in the morning will, nine times out of ten, be all dimples and smiles and mighty bear hugs when you walk through the door at night.

This approach to problems works just as well the other way. Shut the door on your office problems when you leave work. After a night at home among people who think you're special, and aren't afraid to show it, you'll find yourself in much better shape to face and put to rout the job problems in the morning.

129

In any case you can't worry about both sets of problems at once. You can't do justice to reading Peter and the Wolf to your six-year-old, while in your head you're going over the corrections in the quarterly report you'll be explaining to your wolf of a boss in the morning. And you can't make an A+ presentation to that new client, if you're thinking about the F Johnny got in math this report card. Especially if you're thinking the F is all *your* fault. Even if part of it is, remember some of it may well be the teacher's fault, and Johnny himself is hardly an innocent bystander.

The thing to do is to worry at the right time, in the right place, about the right thing. (Don't ever worry about things you can't do anything about.) You may think only a robot or a monster could compartmentalize her feelings and worries so mechanically. Not true. The people who do are not robots or monsters—they're the people who live all the lives they're capable of and interested in. And do it well. *And* have a marvelous time.

People like that seem to have one special talent they're either born with or developed at an early age—the art of handling stress and emotional problems. I suspect the place they start is with those two little words—Know Thyself.

Know what's natural to you. Just as each of us has a natural weight that's healthiest for us, we each have our own best energy-expenditure rates. Maybe a friend can pack ten things into her day, but your energy expenditure rate may not allow for that. Remember too, one person's stress is another person's stimulus.

If you're having problems, it helps to know the underlying pattern. You have to recognize what's happening—and why—before you can figure out what to do about it. One useful question to keep asking yourself from time to time is, "Are my standards of achievement and excellence relevant *for me at this time?*" The answer may be "No" more often than you think.

Relief from stress and worry is as important as relief from chores. Indecision is a wasting—and wasteful—emotional burden. It's often cheaper, emotionally speaking, to be wrong than undecided. At least when you've made a mistake, you've learned something. When you haven't decided, you're still at Square One.

Stress sends signals loud and clear. One is overeating. Another is drinking too much. A third is sleep problems. One doctor says you're probably under stress if you fall asleep easily, wake up three hours later, and can't get back to sleep. The most common symptom of all is constant fatigue. (Ever notice that happy people never seem to be tired?) Even if the symptoms are not physical, if stress is chronic, it'll show up in some other area, from poor job performance to marital problems. Leave it to the Japanese—those wizards of productivity—to meet the problem head on. They schedule yoga breaks during the working day and reserve rooms where employees can throw dishes.

As one study has shown, the people most satisfied with their free time (least likely to feel stress) are those who occasionally feel rushed, only occasionally have time on their hands. They've found the ideal degree of structure within which to handle freedom.

This is how my friend Lynn puts it: "I go through periods where I'm under a great deal of stress, then very little. It's that undulating part that works well for me. I like that style. I need the stretching dimension. It's knowing your limitations. It's pacing yourself as far as the timing of when you put yourself under the stress rather than eliminating stress totally. Not overloading the circuits. I like to live the passioned life. I like the excitement, turmoil sometimes. I like coming out of that, too. The resolution."

Another encouraging bulletin from the front comes from a recent General Mills study showing that mothers who work have better communication within the family. The assertiveness women are learning in the office is helping them deal with children at home. And once your own self-esteem increases, you'll expect more from others.

There are those who feel that the secret of survival for a working woman is to do one thing at a time and to make sure it's *well done.* Well, yes—and no. It depends. Most of my clients feel as I do that we'd never get where we want to go if we really did only one thing at a time. Life isn't long enough. Yet there's no surer way to feel frazzled, put upon, furious, and inept than to keep doing two or more things at once—badly.

How to do
two things at once

The trick is to pair the right two things. Two things you can do at once *and* well. Sometimes you stumble upon them by happy accident. As, for instance, one of my clients did when her oldest daughter was nine years old. She was at an age when she loved to read aloud to her mother, but with several younger children in the family mother could only find the time by continually postponing

131

household chores until she found herself doing the dishes at midnight. In desperation one day, she said, "Why don't you read to me while I do the dishes?" Her daughter pulled up a chair 2 feet away from the sink and read uninterruptedly for thirty to forty-five minutes every night. One is not forced into doing dishes badly when one is being read to, and one doesn't listen badly because one is doing the dishes. On the other hand, being read to by your nine-year-old while you are trying to get your two-year-old ready for bed is a losing proposition leading to annoyance and frustration on all sides.

Here is a starter list of doing-two-things-at-once that work well:

Read the evening paper in the same room where the children are watching their TV show.
Discuss family matters while eating dinner together.
Talk on the phone to a friend while doing your nails.
Do your mending and ironing while watching your favorite TV show.

Two-things-not-to-do-at-once list   Here is a list of doing-two-things-at-once booby traps that should be avoided at all costs:

1. Don't plan a party for the evening of a workday. (Why double the pressure and halve the fun?)
2. Don't eat while you work. (No one can look "in charge" with her mouth full.)
3. Don't try to watch TV with your children and chat with your visiting mother-in-law at the same time. (That kind of togetherness makes everybody wish they were apart.)
4. Don't start a diet and stop smoking at the same time. (You're not *really* a masochist, are you?)
5. Don't shop for clothes on the same day you have to be somewhere for an important date right afterwards. (Why risk arriving tired, disgruntled, and late?)
6. Don't try to reorganize a closet while you're cleaning the house. (One or the other won't be finished—and the one that's finished won't be done right.)
7. Don't try to talk on the phone to your office and keep an eye on your toddler at the same time. (She can wander out of sight and into trouble faster than you can say, "Please hold on.")

8. Don't plan to shop for dinner on the way home every day during a week when you're on a crash project at the office. (Last minute meetings will cross you up every time.)

9. Don't try to eat and shop on the same lunch hour. (You won't do either very well.)

10. Don't try to write checks while your husband—or anyone—is trying to fill you in on his day. (Neither he nor the bank will be happy.)

11. Don't do anything that needs concentration—study, read a book, do a report—while the children are around. (The only kind of concentrating that works around kids is on the kids.)

12. Don't invite an important guest over on a Sunday when it's your husband's day to relax with the newspaper or football on TV. (Neither your guest nor your husband will have a good time.)

13. Don't raise unresolvable issues with your husband while getting ready to go out for a lovely evening. (While lovely evenings may end in unlovely arguments, unlovely arguments never lead to lovely evenings.)

14. Don't help the kids with their homework at the same time you raise behavior problems. (It's hard for them to feel grateful and mad at the same time.)

15. Don't cook a gourmet meal while involved in a project in another room. ("A watched pot never boils"—but an unwatched bouillabaisse always boils over.)

16. Don't get dressed and feed the kids at the same time. (A dollop of oatmeal has never been the right finishing touch for a designer dress.)

17. While you're angry at your husband, don't get involved in any discussion where your objective opinion will be needed. (It won't be objective.)

Don't spend your energy on housework

Don't think of how much housework you can get done—but how little you can get by with. Of all kinds of work, housework is the most awesome example of Parkinson's Law: Work expands to fill the time available.

If you want to allot twenty-four hours a day to doing housework, you'd have no trouble finding things that could be done to make the place look better. Not only because there's an almost limitless supply of jobs to do—washing floors, cleaning closets, scrubbing off finger marks, dusting venetian blinds, tidying drawers, polishing silver—but because almost all of them need doing again very soon—in a matter of days, or if you have children, in hours.

"As little as you can get by with" does not mean living in a mess. Messy surroundings do not save energy—they waste it. Any energy you think you've saved by not doing the work is used up in feeling guilty and depressed, never being able to find anything, and feeling uptight when somebody drops in.

Even if you live alone, and there's nobody around to raise an eyebrow at the chaos, coming home day after day to dishes in the sink and unmade beds does not give a lift to your spirits or improve your self-image. Yet you're right in feeling you can't hold a full-time job, have time for rest and relaxation, and live up to the housekeeping standards of your house-proud mother.

The business approach to housework

Put your efforts where the payoff is biggest—refuse to spend a smidgen on areas offering little return. In other words, train yourself in "selective housekeeping." The cleanest bedroom will look dirty if the bed isn't made. The spotless kitchen will look seedy if there are dishes in the sink. You may have vacuumed and dusted the living room only yesterday, but if the papers and magazines are strewn all around, it will look as if you hadn't bothered to clean it in a month.

Clean is ideal—but it takes time. Clutter is what does you in and you can get rid of it in minutes. Make the bed in five, do the dishes in ten, pick up papers and magazines in no time at all and you've saved yourself hours of serious cleaning.

Put a small bowl or two of flowers in a room and people won't notice you haven't dusted. Even if they do, they'll forgive you.

Make the children responsible for keeping their rooms in some semblance of order. If they don't, just keep their doors shut.

If you find you can't seem to keep things neat no matter how hard you try, don't assume you've got a flawed character. Maybe you've got a flawed environment.

"When Mark and I were first married," one of my clients told me, "I was so impressed with his neatness and sense of organization, it gave me a permanent inferiority complex. We lived in a one-bedroom apartment till our first child was two years old. We had to share the one big closet, but each of us had our own chest of drawers.

"His suits were always beautifully hung in the closet and his shirts, socks, and so on, neatly laid out in the drawers. My dresses were always falling off the hangers or hung up on hooks, and my bureau drawers were a mess. And each year, I felt I was getting worse, instead of improving.

"I didn't really figure out what the matter was until we moved to a larger apartment where we each had our own closet and the baby had a room of her own. Almost overnight my character was transformed. My closet was as neat as his and so were my bureau drawers.

"In the old days, because his suits took up so much room and were so heavy for me to move aside, my dresses were always squashed at one end of the closet. It was a hassle every time I wanted to take one or put it back, so I took to hanging them on hooks or draping them over a chair so I could get at them easily. And my bureau drawers were a jumble because I had only two compared to his four. The bottom two were all crammed with the baby's gear.

"Now the baby's stuff is all in her room, I have a whole closet to myself, a whole chest of drawers too—and you wouldn't believe I was the same woman. Talk about neat and organized!"

We can't always live in a big house or spacious apartment, but we can avoid the erosion of our self-esteem and the chronic irritation that stems from too little space. If you have to move a stack of books every time you need a little elbow room, get another bookcase. If you're running out of desk space, get a file cabinet for all those papers. If your kitchen is so cramped you have to lift four items to get the one you're after, put up some hanging shelves.

All of this may be so obvious, you may wonder why I'm making such a point of it. The reason is women tend to put up with things rather than change them. We put up with annoyance and difficulty and inconvenience instead of taking the time and making the effort to get rid of the problem at the root. It takes time and money to go buy a bookcase or file cabinet or shelves for the kitchen. But once you've done it, you've saved yourself hours and days and months of annoyance and inefficiency and wasted effort. You wouldn't put up with it at work. You'd complain to management. At home, *you're* management.

In these days of conserving precious natural resources, you wouldn't let a dripping faucet go on for months, it would be too great a waste. Your energy too, is a precious natural resource and you shouldn't let it go to waste in dozens of constant little leaks.

In sum, spending your energy wisely is not so much a matter of remembering specific little "must dos" and "don't dos" as understanding the basic strategy of energy efficiency and making it second nature in everything you do.

As one efficiency expert says, "It's more important to do the right thing than to do things right."

That means always having your priorities straight. Get into the habit of doing things in the right order, not only in big tasks but in small ones. Just as you do the research before you write the report, you line up the babysitter before you choose the night to give the dinner party—not after.

Whatever you're doing, follow the First Commandment in sports: Keep Your Eye On The Ball. Glance away at the crucial moment and you miss. It's just as true of work as of games. It's the little moments of inattention that lead to sloppiness, that make the finished job worse than you know you can do, *and* that make work for yourself. You didn't notice and now you've sewn the lining behind the button in a clump. Your little one is screaming because you looked away just as she was reaching for the glass and now the milk is spilled all over the floor.

When you've finished a big project—at work or at home—it helps to summarize it, even briefly, for a running start next time. Jot down what happened, who your contacts were, what the conclusions or recommendations were, how you'd do it next time.

HOW TO GET MORE ENERGY WHEN YOU NEED IT

Important as it is to save energy in every way you can—and to spend it wisely—it's even more important to know where you can lay your hands on more when you need it.

Energy is a working woman's capital. It's probably as crucial to her success as brains, education, talent, and charm. If you're skillful, you can often put one asset in place of another when one is in short supply. Brains will often make up for the lack of a good education, and talent will get you a lot of forgiveness for inexperience, but almost nothing can take the place of energy.

Think of the successful working women you know, and no matter how varied their backgrounds, their careers, their lifestyles, chances are the one thing you'll find they have in common is high energy. It helps to be born with it, but even if you're not, there's a lot you can do to increase your natural reserves. In the process you may discover you have more energy to be tapped than you dreamed of.

You have two kinds of energy to draw on—physical and psychic. The physical is grounded in good health—nutrition, exercise, rest. All those boring things your mother has been telling you about since you were little. If you always let it go in one ear and out the other as most of us do while we're growing up, perhaps it's time for a little review.

Two kinds of energy

Plain, old-fashioned health has never had more going for it. Healthy is In. Fitness is in flower. Vitality is of the Essence. Pale and wan is not romantic—it's dreary. Spending the winter with sniffles is not chic. Stumbling from one day to the next in a fog of fatigue is not heroic—it's bad planning.

Healthy is "in"

Yet who among us hasn't allowed herself to fall into such states of disrepair from time to time? In fact, who has a better set of excuses than the average working woman, wife or mother? Hardly anybody—conceded. But if we settle for excuses, instead of changing what needs to be changed, we're not going to live the way we'd like to and neither will the people who live with us.

This is my friend Gail speaking. "I am just drinking hot water now because I was drinking eight cups of coffee a day last spring. I lost my appetite and just existed on cookies and coffee . . . everything piled up in one week—deadlines on the job, big events in the family and in my social life. I had a head-on collision with myself—my body crashed into itself, I felt sick and nauseous and depressed. It lasted one week. When I quit caffeine I had nausea and headaches as part of my withdrawal. I was so anxious about what was coming up in my life I didn't need the caffeine at all. With my own metabolism

137

generating enough adrenaline, I probably never need coffee. I missed the inside warmth, holding it in my hands, giving me the excuse for a pause—so I ask for tea, but without the teabag."

Working women, wives or not, can't afford to be sick. If you're single, you have to cope alone, which is only added stress. If you have a husband and/or children, you're all, in a sense, sick together. Because you know how to take care of them better than they know how to take care of you.

If you think this health craze is just that—a fashionable madness—don't dismiss it so lightly. Don't dismiss it at all. Make room for the essentials of it in your life. Especially the two elements you're most likely to shortchange yourself on—exercise and rest. If the savviest male executives can find time for regular workouts, so can you.

Whether it's jogging before breakfast three times a week, or racquet ball on your lunch hour, or walking home from work instead of taking the bus, the time you make for exercise will pay you three times over in the extra energy reserve it builds for you. If you have a lethargic metabolism you'll do better on very active release. High metabolism is better off with relaxing exercises. And if you are one of the few lucky ones who have a body with natural muscle tone and energy, then at least balance your activity with enough rest.

"I never had a weight problem," says Gail, "so I never forced myself to make a habit of exercise. My internist says you can run on adrenaline till forty, but after that you pay a high price for no exercise."

Give yourself the breaks

You need to take breaks. Regularly. Schedule them. It's the only way you'll really get them. They're not just indulgences—they're lifesavers.

"When I was single," says Barbara, "whenever I was tired I used to take a weekend off. I'd go home from work, bring home food, close the door, sleep, eat, not talk to anybody. And that was my vacation. I know when I've had enough. I know how to take care of myself.

"Now when my three kids get into bed—eight P.M.—I get into bed. It's my time. I get undressed and sit. Don't do anything. Don't like to think at night. I turn myself off. It's my recuperation. I read magazines, watch TV, sleep at ten or eleven."

"I always remember a cartoon I saw once," another friend said to

138

me. "It showed a middle-aged man in pajamas sitting on the edge of his bed in the morning, saying to his wife forlornly, 'Well, I guess it's time to get up and let 'em at me.' I identified."

After years of hurtling through early morning breakfasts with her large family, she has for some years been getting to work an hour early so she can sit in peace in the company cafeteria (beautifully clean, carpeted, and quiet), have her coffee and English muffin, and read the *New York Times* front to back for a whole uninterrupted hour. "As long as I've had that hour," she says, "I can 'let 'em at me' with anything they've got for the rest of the day on the job. I know I can handle it."

Your psychic energy, too, can be depleted. If life always seems to be "more of the same" in work . . . in environment . . . in clothes . . . in activities. But there are ways to stop that energy drain as well.

You can recharge your psyche in all sorts of ways. Variety. Beauty. Surprise. Instead of marking time till your vacation, do something a little different in your *normal* routine. But above all, do something nice for yourself.

How to give your psyche a boost

One client redecorated her dressing area to make it as pretty and revitalizing as possible. She got rid of clutter, surrounded herself with her favorite color, photos of happy family events, flowers, and her favorite potpourri. It's her personal retreat—the one place in the house that's all her own, exactly the way she likes it. Everybody needs a place where she can spend some time in an environment that's uniquely hers—not the result of the endless compromises family living or the workplace usually demand.

Another friend gets through her roughest times with one simple formula. "No matter how tired I am," she says, "I won't let the day close down on me until I've had a chance to do at least one thing I *want* to do. Even sleep won't make up for the eighteen-hour days when you haven't had a chance to do one thing except what you *had* to do. Even if my eyes are closing, I'll read a chapter in a book I care about . . . or look at Johnny Carson . . . or take one more shot at the crossword puzzle. If you get a whole string of days with nothing but 'musts,' with no room for a single 'want,' you really begin to feel depressed, malnourished, and, inevitably, *mad*. Making room for at least one 'want' eases up the pressure."

Dot your day with little pleasures and satisfactions. They can add up to a happy outlook—a whole that's a lot more than the sum of its parts. Even the simple things—a flower in the bathroom or a gift abloom with bows in a favorite color—can be nourishment for the spirit, food for the eye.

Reward yourself for finishing a difficult or boring job at home—even for getting started on something you've dreaded. I find a good way to make myself take the plunge into a job I've been avoiding is to plan the reward and work backward. I arrange to meet my friend Liz at the little sidewalk cafe around the corner two hours from now, and work like crazy to make the deadline. Then I have *two* things to feel good about—getting the job done, and the chance to trade shop talk over croissants and coffee.

REWARDS AND REFRESHERS

- Buy a bunch of flowers for your bedroom or bath.
- Look for a small pretty accessory to add a touch of glamour to outfits you're bored with.
- Take time out once a month to lunch with a friend—there's nothing more therapeutic.
- Feel proud of having respect for yourself by refusing that dessert or second drink.
- Every once in a while go for a manicure or pedicure, facial, massage, etc.—whatever gives you the biggest lift.
- Have a break-the-routine movie date with your husband on Wednesday nights.
- If you have flexible hours, take off early one afternoon a month to browse the stores and galleries, even to sit in the park and read.
- Get your hair cut in a great new style.
- Take a bubble bath with bath oils.
- Buy a beautiful blouse.
- Buy a new lipstick.
- Change your typical outfit. If you're always wearing pants, wear a dress.
- Stop in for a drink after work with a friend at a relaxing place with atmosphere.
- Spend time with a happy person.

- Take a dance class.
- Drive to your errands with great music playing.
- Break any pattern that feels like a rut (your routine).
- Change your room refresheners often. Use them in closets too, if potpourri is too expensive.
- Relax with radio in bathroom while having your bath. A relaxing bath helps you think about caring for yourself.

If you're not sure you can keep all the foregoing helpful hints always in mind, I can give you the single basic one that will get the same result they're all aimed at. *Think of yourself as a Mercedes.*

If your family were lucky enough to have a beautiful, powerful Mercedes, it wouldn't make sense for them to keep it permanently in the garage so nothing could happen to it and it would always be there when they wanted it. On the other hand, it would be criminal to drive it without let-up, without care, as if it were totally indestructible, regardless of neglect. When it was finally kaput, the family would suffer even more than the car. They would be without vital transportation, without a beautiful and prized asset they could depend on and take pride in.

Too many working women view themselves and treat themselves like a family jalopy—the last item to be paid attention to, so long as it still goes. The trouble with thinking of yourself like that is that you start *acting* like that. Instead of purring along life's freeways, you're wheezing, creaking, and stalling out on local streets, looking scruffy, unpolished, untaken care of. You lose and they lose.

It needn't happen—and it won't. Especially if you take the next section to heart—and organize your family.

ORGANIZING YOUR FAMILY (IT'S NOT IMPOSSIBLE!)

For you, as a working woman, your family can be your biggest energy drain—or your surest personal power source. Which one it is is largely in your hands, or more accurately, in your attitude.

If you think of your job as a threat to your family . . . a siphoning

Energy drain or power source?

off of the energy and attention that rightfully belongs to them . . . a personal asset that benefits you more than them, you will find all your energy being used up trying to compensate for all that guilt. And your family will take their cue from you. If *you* feel you're cheating them, it's very easy for them to start agreeing with you.

Your job and family benefits
Concentrate instead on what benefits come to your family *because* you're working—and even how much worse off they'd be if you weren't.

To start with the basics—there's the money. Today most women work because they have to. They're single, divorced, or widowed. Or single parents trying to supplement child support payments. Or wives trying to help husbands reach their mutual goals—a house, a graduate degree, a family—that a single income just can't cover in these days of inflation.

Whether the money you earn is a family bail-out . . . a boost to your living standards . . . or just a shot in the ego, it is an asset to the whole family, both now and in the long run. It's better for your husband to know you can manage on your own if anything happens to him. (Better for you to know that, too.) And better for the children as well. "My husband is very proud, because now it's the thing to do—to have a wife who's successful. He likes having a wife who can really help him with his problems," says my friend Jean.

Then there's the happier, more self-confident, more "with it" you. "My self-esteem and definition of myself are better now than five years ago," says Lynn, "because of life experiences, professional challenges I've taken." If you love your job and the satisfaction it brings, it does nice things for you as a person, which in turn does nice things for your family. A happy, if harried, mother is generally preferred over an unhappy, unharried mother, though staying at home is no guarantee of being unharried. It's often just being harried in a different way—with more time to worry about more trivial things.

There's the plus of raising more self-reliant children. "My kids say, 'Get a job already, Mom. This is too much!'" Children's own sense of themselves as competent, able to cope, develops faster as they understand they're being trusted with more responsibility for themselves and for each other. (It hardly needs saying this doesn't mean they're left on their own, without supervision.) It's just that they understand what a contribution they're making to the family in helping working parents feel at ease about working. Children who are used to being taken care of by loving adults in addition to their parents—nursemaids, sitters, grandmas, etc.—are often likely to be more open and outgoing and at ease with people. My friend Kay had another reason for working. "My two-year-old daughter told me, 'You can't go to work. Daddy works. Mommy cleans house.' I decided I had to fake it for her sake, for her role model."

There are pitfalls, of course. Like nagging. Expecting too much from your spouse, household help, children, yourself. Getting so bogged down in the "musts" you don't have either the time or the energy for the "wants" of both your family and yourself.

Few things in life are more depressing than nagging—for the nagger as well as the naggee. Even the most dedicated nagger must sometime wail to herself, "I was meant for something better than this." (And that goes double for the naggee.) *Nagger or naggee?*

Whichever you are, you're both right. Nagging is usually a sign that something's wrong with the situation—more than the people involved. And the situation can usually be fixed if you look at it long and hard enough. Better yet, it can be prevented.

Nagging sprouts and spreads when people have different standards of performance and expect more of each other than the other is willing to give. Many of the good advice articles will tell you to start reforming the *person*—either yourself or somebody else.

This would not be a bad idea *if* (1) it didn't take so long, (2) the other person was willing to "go first," and (3) you knew how to do it. I have found you often get better results by reforming the environment, rather than the person.

The first step is to get the best help you can find—and afford. Whether you need a full-time nursemaid housekeeper for your two preschoolers or a cleaning woman half a day every other week for you and your husband . . . *spend the money*. This is not an extravagance or a cop-out. It's smart planning, family protection, health insurance—the difference between serenity and a sunny disposition on *Paid help— it's worth it*

143

the one hand, and tension and temper punctuated with all too frequent blow-ups on the other.

Businessmen do not take to doing the typing themselves, parceling it out to each other when finances are tight for the business. They know if they're going to stay in business at all, much less thrive, they need somebody else to do all that, so they can do what brings in the money. Your family is an enterprise also and deserves equally responsible judgment to keep it flourishing.

Give your help crystal clear instructions as to what you want done—and then get that job off your mind. If your instructions aren't clear, you'll not only be annoyed by a badly-done job, you'll be angry at yourself for being an inept manager and wasting the money without getting what you paid for. If you allow your mind to be cluttered by the job you've given someone else, you won't be able to concentrate on your own.

It is better to spend a couple of hundred dollars for a dishwasher, if you're a working couple, than to wrangle over who's going to do the dishes piled up in the sink several times a week. Even if you're both working so hard you're hardly ever in the apartment except to sleep, sooner or later it will get dirty, laundry will have to be done, the bathroom will have to be scrubbed, the kitchen will have to be mopped, and one of you will want the other to do something about it. If one of you caves in and does it, neither of you will be happy. The caver-in will be mad that he caved in—especially if it was the third time in a row—and the other will be annoyed that after all the wrangle, it was done grudgingly.

If you still feel guilty about hiring outside help, try to think what else you could spend the money on that would save you more annoyance or bring more peace and comfort to the household. The treacherous thing about housework hangups is that they make you feel bad three ways: bad about yourself (you're a rotten homemaker), bad about him (he's lazy, selfish, and inconsiderate), and bad about the house (you never feel good about letting anybody in).

But what if there really is no good household help available—and even if there were, you simply don't have the money? There are still things you can do about the environment that will make things easier for the whole family and therefore for you.

144

Change things, not people. Unless you're a born teacher, psychologist, evangelist or such, with lots of patience and natural talent for motivating people, you'll find it a lot easier to change things, routines, environments, than to change people. You can change your physical setup in a day—changing people takes longer. Changing a room to make it easier to clean takes an hour or two—changing your husband's ideas about *his* cleaning can take months.

Regardless of how long it takes to change his mind, changing the room is still a good idea. It will cut your cleaning time, if *you're* still stuck doing it. It will make it easier to persuade him to share the cleaning if he sees it's only a matter of half an hour instead of two hours. And it will even be easier to get good paid help when you can afford it.

One of my clients kept her excellent housekeeper twelve years because the woman said she could clean all eight rooms to her *own* finicky standards in one day, and still have time for a cup of tea and for watching *As The World Turns*. When the family grew up and my client didn't need Annie full time, she was glad her neighbor next door, living in an identical house, wanted to take her on.

Annie tried for a few weeks, but then said she couldn't do it on a permanent basis—it hurt her back too much. My friend was mystified. Was there that much heavy cleaning to do? "It isn't that," Annie said, "It's all that dusting." In every room on every surface there were dozens of framed pictures of the children, trophies of swimming meets, football triumphs, camp awards, knickknacks, etc. It took Annie longer to clean two rooms next door than it took to clean half the house my friend had.

Sooner or later, you're going to have to get down to the serious business of apportioning work and responsibility. How well you manage to do this will depend a great deal on how much work and responsibility you can get rid of *before* you start apportioning.

Is it likely that your thirteen-year-old will do a bang-up job of cleaning the bathroom if that includes picking up and dusting each of the twelve perfume bottles on the open shelf, along with the combs and nail scissors and jars of face creams and curler caddies and twenty-four other cosmetic items on full display? And if she doesn't, will you be able to watch the dust accumulate week after week with no trace of annoyance on your brow? And if you can't, is it worth the running squabble every week to get her to do it to your standard of tidiness? Or is it simple wisdom to put the whole collection in a drawer or in the medicine cabinet, where it won't have to be dusted by her, or you, or anyone?

Before you call a family conference to decide who is to be responsible for what chores, go through room by room and see what jobs can be eliminated or greatly simplified by rearranging the environment. If something is on display, decide if you—or anyone else—likes to look at it enough to be willing to dust it, or shine it, or polish it every week. And if no one likes it that much—not even you—put it away. It's probably been there all those years from sheer habit.

You may be amazed to discover how much work and family argument can be eliminated by this simple exercise. Once you're down to bedrock—the chores that won't go away unless *somebody* does them—the smartest way to assign them is to let everybody do what he/she most likes to do. Carol hates to cook, loves to paint furniture. Her husband loves to cook, loathes paintbrushes. At their house you never hear anyone complain about working their fingers to the bone over a hot stove or a stiff paintbrush.

Susan, an accountant, is married to Tony, an art director. Not surprisingly, she keeps the family books, and he does the interior decorating. As a result, both their finances and their decor—to say nothing of their dispositions—are the envy of their friends.

There is one small trap to be avoided here. It's very easy to load up one person unfairly because "you do it so much better than I." Under that system almost all wives would be back to square one doing all the housework since girls have been nudged into doing it from an early age. They're better at it in most cases through experience, not necessarily talent or inclination.

Here we come to the "below bedrock" level—chores *everybody* hates that *have* to be done. Probably the best way to handle these is by rotation, by lot, or by a point system. (Ten points for cleaning the john, eight for fighting with the electric company, three for baling the magazines for paper pickup, etc.) Add them all up, divide by the number of people in the family, and that is the number of points each person has as his quota for the week.

Chores
everybody hates

The big energy-saver here is taking the resentment off everybody's back. Nobody feels cheated, nobody feels put-upon, and nobody is stuck with being the family policeman, keeping everybody toeing the line.

If your husband is truly liberated, you don't have to read this part. You could probably write it. If your husband is unliberated—and not even trying—but you love him anyway, how do you handle that? Very, very slowly.

*What kind
of husband
do you have?*

Perhaps it would help if you think of him as having a hereditary disease. (In a way, he has.) You wouldn't be angry at him for that . . . that would be pointless. You wouldn't be constantly throwing it up to him . . . that would be cruel. You'd try to help him compensate for it. And you'd keep yourself as healthy, fit, and cheerful of mind as possible to cope. Remember that comforting old maxim about little drops of water wearing away stone . . . so, in gentle little ways, keep trying to bring him into the twentieth century.

Actually, the real challenge is the husband most of us are married to—the one who's long on liberated thinking, but short on liberated acting. He's the one who broils a terrific steak, but leaves the onion-slicing to you. (To say nothing of cleaning the broiler.) Who clips the hedge, and leaves the sweeping up to you. Who paints the bathroom after *you* get the paint and take down the curtains and wash the light fixture, and leaves it to you to put away the ladder and clean the brushes and scrub the floor. Who thinks all the chores are evenly divided when he does the glory part, and you do the gunk part.

While it's worth weaning him away from this lopsided view of things as early as possible, it's not worth grinding your teeth to powder or coming down with a migraine in the meantime. Keep in

147

mind that this is just a carryover from the business world where he has spent most of his life functioning with a total support system, so it's hard for him to notice anything strange about it.

You could insist that turnabout is fair play—but you may find that he will do the gunk part much less well than he does the glory part, and definitely less well than you do. Which means you'll have to live with it as is, or wind up doing it yourself. Perhaps a more sensible way to size up the situation is to think in terms of time saved, rather than fairness achieved.

Choices usually boil down to one of these:

Glory his—gunk yours	Job done: very well. Time saved: considerable Feelings, his: pride and relief Feelings, yours: chronic low-grade annoyance
You do it all—glory *and* gunk	Job done: first-class. Time: twice as long Feelings, yours: pride, exhaustion, resentment Feelings, his: lonesomeness, superfluity, twinge of guilt (maybe), sly satisfaction at getting out of the whole thing
You divide the glory and the gunk between the two of you	Job done: glory part, great; gunk part, half great Time saved: nil—all eaten up by initial negotiation Feelings, his: mad and bewildered Feelings, yours: glad and exhausted

One of the most difficult things to sort out when you're a working woman with a family is just how much you have a right to expect from your husband and children. Support and cooperation? At least. Sacrifice of time, money, freedom, service? Probably. Change of attitude, behavior, lifestyle? Possibly. Change of beliefs, interests, use of free time? Highly unlikely.

What can you expect?

First off, whatever you think you have a "right" to expect, it's better to expect too little than too much. It's the difference between being happily surprised and bitterly disappointed. Second, it's wise to give notice in advance of what you *do* expect—or more accurately— "hope for." Then they'll at least have an inkling and won't have to wonder why you're so out of sorts when there seems to be no discernible reason. Third, and this is absolutely crucial, when they fail to live up to your expectations, as they undoubtedly will, at least in some areas—don't confuse this failure with "They don't really love me."

It's perfectly possible for your husband to love you deeply and sincerely and still refuse to carry out the garbage . . . or get his own dinner three nights in a row . . . or resent the fact that you can't play tennis on Saturday and have dinner at the club because you've got to get out that report for the boss over the weekend.

Can this be love?

What you're up against is not so much lack of love as lack of maturity, lack of awareness, reluctance to change, and perhaps a basic mind-set so ingrained, he couldn't change it if he wanted to. Changed circumstances do help people mature . . . do increase their understanding . . . do encourage change, but with all the luck you could hope for, there's still a point where the person remains as he is and always will be. And you have to decide whether what you love him for outweighs what he can't give you because it isn't in him to give.

Once you've come to that point, you may be surprised at how much tension disappears, how many wrangles and arguments don't occur, and best of all, how many other people and places you can look to, to get what you can't get from him. This is not to say you love him any the less. It's just that you rail at him less and explore other means of filling some of your needs.

149

Two little words to make a working woman's life work: "Think Ahead." As soon as you become a mother, you automatically think ahead to protect your child's life and your own sanity. Thinking ahead is your most effective defense against the dangers and surprises of your daily life. But too many of us don't apply this all-purpose simplifier to our lives in general and ourselves in particular. Here are just a few examples my friends and I have learned to count on over the years.

Basic survival kits
- Have a supply drawer of sharpened pencils, colored pens, various size notepads, stapler, paper punch, paper clips, carbon paper, White-Out, tape, stamps. Get an automatic pencil sharpener. Keep a pad and pencil next to each phone.
- Have a complete tool box.
- Have a well-stocked sewing kit, with iron-on patches, iron-on seam binding for hems, name tapes.
- Have a jar of loose change and tokens.

Master records
- Make up a notebook where you can keep all family data, facts, numbers you need. Things like bankbook numbers, safety deposit box key number, charge account numbers, insurance policy numbers, etc.
- Make important lists to keep handy: Phone numbers of emergency sitters (at least five); prevacation phone call list; kennel, mailman, newspaper delivery, etc., list of staples to check before marketing, a packing list for each member of the family to check before a trip, dates to have the car serviced, all emergency phone numbers.
- Have permanent typed instructions for sitters. Also, room-by-room cleaning instructions for cleaning women.

- Write all dates on a large wall calendar in a different color pen for each family member. That way every member knows what every other member is doing when.
- Make dentist, health checkup, eye exam appointments for children and all family members and plan around them.
- Reorder before you run out of stationery, checks, subscriptions.
- Repair your dying air conditioner in March.
- Put reminder on your calendar to give yourself two weeks to get your mother-in-law's birthday present.

Date doings

- Load up on hostess gifts.
- Load up on small "rewards" for kids—stationery store items they'd love.
- Buy stockings, underwear, kids' socks, husband's handkerchiefs a dozen at a time.

Bulk buying

- Join the AAA.
- Contact the local taxi service and introduce them to the kids in case of emergency.

Lifesavers

- Teach kids simple cooking.
- Cook several of the same favorite meals at once and freeze them.
- Buy a night-before coffee pot—assign someone else to prepare it (housekeeper or your child for 10¢ fee a night.)
- Keep snacks available in the refrigerator or on the shelves so that the children can reach for them themselves.

Shortcuts

- If you've got to keep tabs on your toddler as she wanders from one room to another, think of some little task you can get done in the room where she is—a button to be sewed on while she's in your bedroom or washing your combs in the bathroom while you're keeping an eye on her in the tub. Never just wait.
- If you work at home, do all your top-priority tasks while the kids are in school. Don't expect to get much thought work done after they come home.

Smart timing

151

- For time of your own, plan to be away from the house. It's hard for children to leave you alone when you're around. (Jean Kerr wrote the bulk of her plays sitting in the family car.)
- Take business shoes to the shoemaker just before your vacation.
- Fold laundry right out of the dryer so it doesn't wrinkle.
- If you're going to a dinner party after work, take your change of clothes with you to save a trip home and escape getting embroiled in the chaos of the household.

7

GO FOR IT!

Women have worked since the world began—in some eras and places alongside the men, in others far removed from them. And in the decades since World War II women have become a taken-for-granted part of the office force and the assembly line.

But never, until now in the '80s, have women tried to achieve what more and more of us seem to have set our minds on: to do work that's taken seriously, among men who take us seriously, and still have and keep the things that have mattered most to us throughout history. A marriage that nourishes and supports our deepest needs. Children we love who love us back—and turn out well. The arts and pleasures of running a home and a social life that challenge our skills and refresh our energies.

If we can bring it off, the world will be a livelier, lovelier place. If not *the* world, *our* world. But to bring it off will take all the creativity and ingenuity we can muster. The old rules and rigidities simply don't work when you're trying to juggle a mix of work responsibilities, home and family, pleasure and ambition that has never been tried before—at least not by large numbers of women. "Formula living" doesn't work anymore, any more than formula dressing.

Developing your true image . . . getting yourself organized . . .

enlisting your family in helping you succeed at what you've chosen to do—these are no small accomplishments. They take intelligence and energy and tact and insight and *drive*. And underpinning them all, an unshakable faith in yourself.

Nobody achieves all that overnight, but when you do, you'll know it. You're hitting your stride with style. And getting the unmistakable high that goes with it.

There's nothing more exhilarating for you and the people who love you. Everyone gets a lift from seeing someone looking terrific, feeling terrific, happy in her life . . . doing the things she likes to do and doing them well. Everyone feels cheered and energized to see someone who hasn't settled for half of what she could do and be . . . hasn't given in to a life of "either . . . or . . ." and hasn't sold her soul to become Superwoman.

But no one gets a bigger lift than you. Because you've tapped into the biggest renewable energy source of all. *You'll know you've beaten the system!*

Start Looking Terrific On and Off the Job. Now!

... with an individual wardrobe plan, worked out especially for you, via computer, by Emily Cho!

Thanks to the computer—here's your chance to get from this leading fashion authority and consultant some of the expert help and guidance that has brought her hundreds of clients. It's all yours for only $24.95, plus postage.

Send in the coupon, and you'll get a wide-ranging, comprehensive questionnaire, filled with the same kind of probing questions Emily Cho uses in her private consultations. You'll enjoy filling it in—indeed, just thinking about the answers may give you a better idea of the dimensions of your wardrobe problems.

You will then receive a written report—complete with clothing illustrations—tailored to your own personality, body, and lifestyle needs. It will show you how to disguise your body faults and enhance your assets. How to stop making clothing mistakes that cost you wasted money, time and self confidence. How to put your best You—your *real* You—forward. Not just now and then, but every day on and off the job. An Emily Cho wardrobe is designed to *work for you*. It's not an indulgence—it will be the wisest investment you'll make this year.

ABOUT THE AUTHORS

Emily Cho is the acknowledged founder of the image consulting industry. Hundreds of clients from top executives to TV personalities to women demanding changes and personal growth, rely on her New York–based personal consulting service, *New Image*

Lectures, corporate seminars, and a family including two young children keep this best-selling author of *Looking Terrific* busy. She is the best endorsement for her own book, *Looking, Working, Living Terrific 24 Hours a Day*.

Hermine Lueders has spent most of her working life as a VP-Copy Head at SSC & B, one of New York's top advertising agencies. She has four children and lives with her husband in Pelham, New York.